THE NARROW PATH TO
EXPANSIVE VISION

Essays on following the light of the
greatest leader who ever lived—Jesus Christ

RD OOSTRA

WESTBOW
PRESS®
A DIVISION OF THOMAS NELSON
& ZONDERVAN

WestBow Press books may be ordered through booksellers or by contacting:

WestBow Press
A Division of Thomas Nelson & Zondervan
1663 Liberty Drive
Bloomington, IN 47403
www.westbowpress.com
844-714-3454

Scripture quotations taken from The Holy Bible, New International Version® NIV® Copyright © 1973 1978 1984 2011 by Biblica, Inc. TM. Used by permission. All rights reserved worldwide.

ISBN: 978-1-6642-8324-4 (sc)
ISBN: 978-1-6642-8325-1 (hc)
ISBN: 978-1-6642-8323-7 (e)

Library of Congress Control Number: 2022920666

Print information available on the last page.

WestBow Press rev. date: 12/8/2022

CONTENTS

To our parents, who taught us the importance of faith, family, and hard work.

To two pastors, Lee Powell and Chad Gilligan, whose thoughts and words are woven into this book. Two men who were the best we have experienced in helping make Sunday sermons relevant to our daily lives.

To our family, Drew, Katelyn, Annalyn, Ellerie, Tyler, Jodi, Carson, Caitlin, and Oliver. You have given us joy beyond words.

To our friend, editor and writer Tim Langhorst, whose talents, insights, and passion are truly amazing and whose fingerprints are on every word.

To my wife, Barbara, your love, friendship, counsel, and warm heart have made our forty-plus-year journey together beautiful.

Enter through the narrow gate. For wide is the gate
and broad is the road that leads to destruction, and
many enter through it. But small is the gate and narrow
the road that leads to life, and only a few find it.
—Matthew 7:13–14

INTRODUCTION

Finding the Leadership Example of Christ in an "All about Me" World

Your word is a lamp for my feet, a light on my path.
—Psalm 119:105

I grew up during the late 1950s and 1960s in a rural community in northwest Iowa called Sioux Center. My mom was a Dutch immigrant, and my dad was a first-generation Dutch immigrant. Given that they were the oldest children of their families, they were both required to work from a young age, and as a result, they never had an opportunity to get a formal education. They were farmers and service workers who were focused on work and didn't really travel outside the community, and in doing that, they provided us with a wonderful life. My wife, Barbara, grew up in the same area, although we didn't actually meet until several years after college. Her brother still owns a farm in Boyden, Iowa, passed down from generation to generation for more than one hundred years. Like our parents, we stayed pretty close to home in our younger years.

We lived in a very sheltered, doctrine-driven world. Pretty much everyone in our area lived that way. Our life was one of Protestant work ethic and Calvinism. As Dutch immigrants, we studied the five core points of Calvinism, which stated: people are simple and flawed, with sinful motives at the core; God chooses those people who will be saved; not everybody is going to be saved; once saved, you are always saved; and those who have genuine faith and who are in a state of saving grace can never lose their salvation.

Biblical scholars have debated this doctrine over time, and several points, such as unconditional election and limited atonement, are considered highly controversial, and those are points I certainly have struggled with throughout my life. But as kids from a Dutch reformation background, we learned and lived these principles. Little did we know that growing up on this narrow path would present numerous challenges as we moved through life. Clearly, not everyone grew up like we did.

Let's be clear. This book is not about growing up in a religious community. It's not to criticize my upbringing; I am actually incredibly thankful for it. It is about my faith and leadership journey in the midst of all the noise in everyday contemporary life and seeking a path to being the person, and the leader, I hoped to be. For me, that was following the leadership example of Jesus Christ.

These principles provide a point of reference, a foundation, for decisions made in life and as an adult working together with all faiths as a business and community leader. In following this biblical frame of reference, in Barb's and my experience, we believed in and practiced—and continue to do so—a Protestant work ethic that included temperance, silence, order, resolution, frugality, industry, sincerity, and justice.

As we grew up, we naively thought everybody was the same way we were. We didn't get much education on what we would encounter when we ventured outside our community. But what we found is that having a strong doctrinal focus, a Christian framework, which helped us think about what we believed in as Christians, doesn't always translate well in a modern society and as a leader in the business world or in the community.

And we sadly found most churches were not helpful.

The challenge for me is and has always been, "What do you believe?" And how do we define, and then live, the narrow path? In Matthew 16:15, Christ asks "Who do you say I am?" It is a question that humans have been trying to answer for thousands of years. Through this book, and through my life's journey, I will be offering some possible answers to that question. However you personally might answer this question, there is one thing that you can't deny. Jesus is as relevant today as he was while he lived—perhaps more so. And he will continue to be for millennia to come.

The dilemma for so many Christians then becomes, how do you understand and then find that bridge that helps ease the tension between the Christian life and the secular world—and, honestly, the tension raised between being a Christian and the organized church and church leadership? As we have moved around, that tension has only become worse for us. For some, this tension is a challenge, but others ignore it either by not thinking about it or avoiding thinking about it, and by compartmentalizing their faith and their work.

In the course of my career as a leader in health care administration in various communities in our country, and most recently as the president and CEO of a national health and well-being organization with more than forty thousand employees serving communities in twenty-eight states, there isn't any education out there I know of that helped us effectively translate Christian belief into a leadership approach that works at the office and keeps faith tenets unchallenged. I know that may sound critical, but my experience with multiple churches, pastors, and the endless content on podcasts, news articles, the internet and social media, and other media all seem lacking when helping to make meaningful connections between our faith and leadership.

There was an occasion a couple of years ago when I was working on several presentations at one time. I had a presentation to a business community in one neat, tall pile, and a stack of files for my Bible study group in another neat and very tall pile. And then the two piles teetered and fell into one combined mess. I was immediately upset that the piles had fallen together, but as I sat back in my desk chair, it struck me hard how these two piles were really one. The *good to great* philosophy of leadership from Jim Collins collided with Jeremiah's scribe, Baruch, who in Jeremiah 45:5 was charged to "seek great things for yourself? Do not seek them." This was not the orderly world from my youth.

What had happened seemed like a tremendous metaphor for the separateness of leadership and faith that has frustrated me throughout my career, and it struck a chord.

This epiphany is one main reason for this book. This is not a book about Calvinism but about the failure of the church to help connect work, life, and our faith. It is about my life's journey in trying to balance and apply the foundation of taking the narrow path in a secular world and a misguided church, and how to follow the leadership example of the greatest leader in history—Jesus Christ.

So where do we turn to find a leadership example in an "all about me" world? There are a ton of leadership books out there—by both secular and Christian experts. And every day it seems like there is yet one more book on leadership to consider. It can be overwhelming for anyone to sift through all the literature on how to develop and create a leadership approach. It's even more challenging for those who are trying to weave their faith into their leadership style. The Christian books on leadership seem to be focused on how pastors and other Christian leaders can enhance their leadership approach with their members. But there is not much available for business leaders or even community leaders to find inspiration. Over my career and particularly as I became president and CEO, I tried to follow the approach of many secular leaders since that seemed the modern thing to do, yet, while the expertise and advice provided in these books and articles has been interesting and useful, something essential was missing.

At a church I was attending several years ago, we had a group of people who had formed a book club focused on leadership. We challenged the group to look at famous secular experts on leadership and leading change, and then we compared key principles in these venerable books to the leadership example of Christ. What we found, over and over, was that Christ lived these leadership concepts thousands of year before some of these experts were even born.

The more we dug into the comparison, the more we found similarities, and that served as another inspiration for the creation of *The Narrow Path to Expansive Vision*. I realized that only way to make sense of it all was to base my leadership approach on Jesus Christ. It is a path that leads to true meaning, a path of faith, and a path that leads to salvation.

Defining "Narrow Path"

When you think about the phrase *narrow path*, you may hear echoes of any number of Bible verses in your mind. Matthew 7:13–15, which is quoted as the inscription for this book, is one example. The path is narrow, and the road is hard.

I suspect that people will translate this verse to define *narrow path* to suggest there is no room for chasing worldly pleasures or self-righteousness. And as a Christian, I believe that is certainly true, although we all enjoy many of our world's pleasures. But walking a narrow path does not mean it has to be a bad thing.

Throughout this book, I will be emphasizing different aspects of what I think it means to follow the narrow path.

Taking the narrow path does not mean you are rigid and narrow-minded. It is the opposite of that. It provides you a framework, a context, a lens for your life narrative that will allow you to have a broader, more inclusive vision for your life purpose. And that is key! It is the ultimate purpose!

Through my journey in in this book, there will be illustrations of people who have taken the concept of the narrow path and used it for their own purposes in order to maintain authority or power and to justify actions that would be far from being Christlike.

Taking the narrow path is about having the discipline and the strength to truly try to follow a Christ-inspired life and leadership approach. It is a life of servant leadership; the last is first, and first is last. Not a world of the "gospel according to me." It is looking at Christ's example of leadership in everything we do, understanding, of course, that this is aspirational, as we are all incomplete as people and leaders.

I will talk extensively about servant leadership in this book, and it is not an easy thing to accomplish. I don't pretend to have all the answers. But it is the compassionate path—sharing the suffering of others. It takes great discipline and sacrifice, and in that sense, it is a narrow path to take.

This is the context in which I will be using the phrase *narrow path* throughout this book. It is a discipline that has opened a gateway that has helped me achieve a more expansive vision in my life. This concept is the rationale for the title of this book, *The Narrow Path to Expansive Vision.* These two goals in life aren't in opposition to each other. They actually work very well together.

While they work together in concept, making this a reality has always been challenging. Throughout my professional career—and in my personal life—I have experienced more than my share of tension between my religious beliefs and business decisions that have been made—and the churches where I have worshiped. To be able to act as a Christ-inspired leader, you have to understand the natural tension between these worlds and how it impacts your ability to continue along a Christ-inspired path in a secular world.

Unfortunately, the church hasn't provided the tools we need to navigate the secular world, and many of the messages from the church don't translate to a work setting. I have heard hundreds of great sermons, but few effectively bridged the connection to my daily life. The church and its leaders have not done a good job of providing a context that our faith life and our work and family life are all the same.

You get in your car on Sunday morning and, however you worship, kind of visualize this driving down a narrow highway to a church. You hear the teaching from the pastor, and maybe you are being exhorted to do something over and above. But on Monday morning when you walk out the door, you jump back onto the broad highway. It is subtle, this gentle slope on the broad highway. And before you know it, you get lulled into an approach that takes you away from the narrow path. The erosion along the broad road happens very quickly. And quickly we compartmentalize our lives. How do we navigate that narrow path as we leave church on Sunday? My experience is that this erosion often leads to frustration and a lack of meaning, including at times a feeling of depression and a sense that we are on our own. Moving away from the narrow path can result in a feeling of loss and a sense of merely running through the motions.

Think about Christ when he encountered the Samaritan woman who had come to draw water from the well. As he comes to understand her story, Christ doesn't take a narrow-minded approach, which would be to tell the woman that she wasn't living the right way and to stop it or go to hell. Christ was more open-minded and said to take a different route, follow a different path, live your life differently. It took tremendous discipline, commitment, and vision to take this path. I don't think narrow-mindedness helps people, and certainly it doesn't help leaders.

Over the years, my wife, Barbara, and I have lived in various parts of the country, and that was always frustrating because, while we looked, it was always difficult if not impossible to find a church that followed the doctrine we were familiar with and that we used in our lives and where we worked. We have met some tremendously positive Christians moving through life, but the concern has always been having the right balance, depth of faith, and faith in action.

We had an opportunity to experience many different types of churches and their philosophies. We have gone to seeker churches, which do bring people to God, but they don't extend much beyond that; rather, it is about feeling good. Here's a Bible, and maybe here are some readings to consider. When you start to evaluate that approach, you think, *Okay, I got that. I feel good. But there has to be something more.*

One of the seeker churches we attended sponsored a leadership series. Instead of focusing on the leadership approach of Jesus, they featured the latest great business leader of the day, like Jack Welch, talking about grading people, firing from the bottom 10 percent—pretty condescending in attitude. Where did that come from? If you screened from a Christian leadership perspective, you would never do anything like that. Jesus didn't judge people. He would say, "Sin no more and go forward." Yet these church leaders were chasing successful secular leaders and hoping that by some process of osmosis, these principles would be emulated by Christian leaders. There was the underlying premise that if Christians were better business leaders, with pastors often encouraging us to follow the advice of secular leaders, then everybody wins.

At one place, Barbara and I found a church similar to our church from our childhood. The church experience was familiar, but the connection to work community and social needs wasn't there. At one point, the leadership of a church we were attending was considering moving their church to a new location. Because my work in health care involves dealing with construction and business and community development, I was asked to help find a new location for the outreach. One great option was an inner-city location near a hospital in our health system. One of the church leaders commented that they didn't want to move there because they should fear that part of the community. I may have misunderstood, but my takeaway was that some wanted to separate from the community. And ultimately, they did move to a building in the suburb far outside the community center. Personally, it was very disheartening and again brought up the challenge we face when churches live outside the real world we often work in. Maybe that wasn't their goal, but the concern is that, as we separate ourselves from our communities, the tendency to ignore the needs of people is increased.

We went to churches that were Christian, Protestant, seeker churches, and many others. And in most cases, the reason we enjoyed the church was not only because of the community but because the pastor had meaningful sermons that we could use on Monday through Saturday, as well as Sunday.

There have been a few pastors we have loved who have a great way of talking about life purpose and meld together life and faith. They talk about things we can use day to day. And that's what we have to do as Christian leaders—and all leaders of faith.

Recent national research continues to point to an increasing decline in ethics, morals, and faith. Based on the May 2-22 Gallup Values and Beliefs poll, a record high of 50 percent of Americans rate the overall state of moral values in the United States as "poor."[1] This is the highest ranking of negative views on the nation's moral values in the decades that Gallup has conducted this poll. The same poll found that Americans' belief in God has dipped to a new low; that percent is still 81 percent, but that is 6 percent down from 2017, and it is the lowest rating since Gallup first asked this question in 1944.[2] And a recent study commissioned by a Pentagon in-house think tank concluded that America is losing many of the seven attributes the research believed were essential for competitive success: national ambition and will; unified national identity; shared opportunity, an active state; effective institutions; a learning and adaptive society; and competitive diversity and pluralism.[3]

What This Book Isn't ... and Is

Let me start first with what this book isn't. It is not intended to be a scholarly, academic discourse on doctrine and debate on the meaning of the Bible or the Gospels. It is not a textural, traditional, reductive, or scholarly review. While many scholarly books and articles were reviewed in writing *The Narrow Path to Expansive Vision*, this book is not intended to be an academic exercise. This book isn't for theologians (or perhaps, really, it is). It's not a debate about faith. It is about finding a practical approach that can shape lives. It is a commentary through the lens of my life experiences and through studying the New Testament and Gospels, viewing Jesus as a leader rather than primarily as a teacher. The book is about my life and leadership journey, striving to follow a Christ-inspired path, struggling to integrate elements of the secular world along the way, and aligning it all with the leadership example of Christ. It is my leadership study, with the intent to provide it as a guide to you as well—and perhaps to apply.

How do you live a narrow-path life in a wide-path world and society? Where do you make compromises? Are there topics you just don't talk about? How do you refocus after you fail? What boundaries do you draw where you say, "I am just not going there"? This book will hopefully help answer some of those questions.

Because this book is about the leadership example of Christ, I will largely focus on the Gospels according to Mark, Matthew, Luke, and John. And even more specifically, I will talk a lot about the Sermon on the Mount and the Beatitudes, both of which have shaped what it means to be a leader and have had a major influence on Western culture throughout written history. The Sermon on the Mount can be found in chapters 5 through 7 in the Gospel of Matthew, and in a similar version in chapter 6 of Luke, called the Sermon on the Plain. Themes Jesus talks about in the Sermon on the Mount are essential attributes for leaders: humility, mercy, love your enemies, and do good to others. The Beatitudes included in the Sermon on the Mount are blessings given by Jesus. While you may not know them as Beatitudes, you almost certainly have heard these blessing, beginning with phrases like "Blessed are the poor in spirit" or "Blessed are the meek." They serve as ideals or values that leaders should use in their leadership approach. The Sermon on the Mount is only a couple of thousand words long—but such powerful words.

Book Organization

My life, along with my wife's, has been a journey from a family- and a community-based philosophy heavy in doctrine to living and working in a secular world and many different types of organized religions. Through that journey, I have tried to develop a Christ-inspired leadership approach that helps me as a leader in business and in the community, as well as striving to be a better spouse, parent, mentor, sibling, partner, citizen, and, most importantly, a better person of faith. I believe everyone should develop their own framework that will help them navigate through their work life. Mine started with a file of articles and books that were my favorites—my go-to resources on leadership. I have changed my framework to add a new thought. Our framework may be Bible based or it may be based on a different framework, but there should be a foundation to help us think about and move forward in meeting the challenges that face us all. This book offers a practical and hopefully meaningful approach to consider.

Each chapter in the book is inspired by one or more of the key components from the Christ-inspired leadership framework, which will be summarized in the final chapter.

Throughout the book, to help illustrate some concepts in Christ-inspired leadership, there will be numerous examples about how the company I led for over thirteen years launched and expanded our healthy equity and social determinants of health program. Social determinants of health are those societal factors such as poverty, hunger insecurity, access to quality food and housing, financial insecurity, systemic racism—all of which have an incredible impact on an individual's health and well-being. In fact, social determinants have far more impact on a person's health than the clinical/medical care they receive. These same social determinants also play a major role in a community's health and well-being. We started with a small project related to hunger, and thirteen years later, we have a nationally recognized, comprehensive focus on addressing health inequity and health disparities. This is an ideal topic and a great example because it all is driven by a philosophy of servant leadership and illustrates how a Christ-inspired leadership can influence the mission of a secular organization. Was this work motivated by personal faith and belief in what Jesus Christ would do—and, in fact, did? Absolutely.

The initial chapters will discuss the process of first seeking a narrow path and establishing the need for a Christ-inspired leadership framework and how I have tried to understand and balance the tension we all feel, both inwardly focused and externally, between the sacred and secular worlds. In addition, I commissioned some original research regarding how leaders in business who identified as being Christian viewed the leadership example of Christ. The results, while maybe not surprising to me, were pretty revealing, and not in a good way.

The next chapters explore how, using my life's journey as an example, we all seek to find purpose and a mission, and then through Christ-inspired servant leadership, we can lead change, develop future leaders, and continue to grow as we gain new and meaningful perspective. As part of the narrative arc of these chapters, I will compare and contrast Christ's leadership approach to some of the most influential secular writings on leadership and leading change over the last fifty years. The similarities between the secular principles of leadership are strikingly similar to how Christ led during his ministry. In particular, the parables in the Gospels, the Beatitudes, and the Sermon on the Mount all anticipate the foundation for contemporary books on leadership.

The final chapter of the book will propose a new model for Christ-inspired leadership.

To be consistent, any Bible verses quoted in this book are from the New International Version of the Bible. If a Bible verse from a different version is used, that will be noted in the citation immediately following the verse.

Who Should Read This Book?

For the last several years, I have given a leadership lecture at a local university, which includes a very diverse audience of mostly younger people, business majors as well as liberal arts majors, Christians and non-Christians. In my most recent leadership academy lecture, I increasingly talked openly about the connection I have with my faith and how that impacts my work, as well as the importance of having a true balance between your work and your home life. I was curious how talking about these connections would go over, but I was pleasantly surprised at the reaction I got from the students; they were very positive about my willingness to talk about the connection between my work and my faith and home life. And I was humbled honestly that they were finding the words I offered to be in some fashion inspiring and that this could be an approach that they should take as they entered the real world. It reinforced the metaphor of my two presentations, one a business script and the other a faith script, falling together in a way that made the two presentations more powerful.

I have found that as I developed and continue to refine this Christ-inspired leadership framework, it has acted as a litmus test or a screen for my behavior in life, at work, and in my community. It serves as my starting point each day. And it is my hope that, through my journey, this Christ-inspired leadership framework can be of benefit to anyone—someone who is exploring their life purpose, someone who is Christian or non-Christian, someone who doesn't have strong faith or any faith at all, or someone who is struggling and is questioning his or her faith. It is ultimately a story about the discipline to take a Christ-inspired path focused on servant leadership to achieve a broad vision. That is Christ's leadership example. And it a leadership story for the ages.

PART 1

Seeking a Narrow Path in a Wide-Path World

O N E

"THE GOSPEL ACCORDING TO ME"

Obliterating Common Ground and Common Language

I have always felt the tension between the sacred and the secular. For me, there was the essence of Calvinism as described in the acronym TULIP (total depravity, unconditional election, limited atonement, irresistible grace, and perseverance of the saints) and the highly structured biblical framework of the narrow path. Unfortunately, the doctrine may help you think about what you believe as a Calvinist Christian, but it doesn't always translate in daily life and how you take those principles to work and in your personal and community life. We all must navigate the noise in our lives, whether we are religious or not.

For Christian leaders, there seem to be two major types of conflicts that contribute to the struggle of how to integrate Christian concepts in leadership while continuing our journey on a narrow path. There is that internal conflict between what is *correct* doctrine and internal enlightenment, focusing on our internal spiritual foundation. Then there are external conflicts, such as the secular versus the sacred and traditional leadership approaches versus Christian-inspired servant leadership approaches. There is also the careful dance in practicing your faith at work.

We find ways to process these conflicts, test them against Christian concepts and values, and live them. There is a lot of self-reflection. The way Barbara and I grew up, right or wrong, we were taught a framework for our belief. And sometimes we struggled with that internally in determining how we were going to take that out into the world, aligning and integrating the reality of the external world with our internal beliefs.

For example, we had a somewhat unfulfilling experience at a seeker church we attended, and in many respects, these types of churches are great places of worship. This church brought a lot of people to Christ. But it didn't really give us a lot of depth in regard to doctrine. While we went there, there were times we felt like they just needed to give additional depth. We didn't really get that, and the leadership of the seeker church made no excuses for it. They were trying to live the Great Commandment to bring as many people to God as possible. While you have to admire their commitment and success, you also can be concerned that these types of churches focus too much on who can have the better coffee bar, who can have the better musical group, and who has the largest numbers. It is those who preach the power of positive thinking, which is great until you run into somebody you don't like at work. What do you do then? These friendly churches seem not to aspire to have any sense of depth, so they provide no real answers or guidelines on how to effectively navigate these types of situations. So either you adapt or you move on.

Through it all, you have to guard against being complacent outside of church. We sleepwalk through the rest of our lives, almost like making a wax statue that could easily melt away. It is easy to fall into a check-the-box mentality. Went to church: check. Said my daily prayer: check. The tools to live our daily lives do exist, but it feels like they have never been integrated completely as that foundation into our lives, not only a purpose in life but also what kind of leadership style or leadership approach to take.

At the leadership academy presentation I mentioned at the end of the introduction, one of the first things I talk about is developing your own leadership point of view because everyone is different. You shouldn't try to be someone else; you should take the time to really have your own point of view. I then go through a series of secular articles that have influenced how I think about leadership (a number of which we will discuss throughout this book). But I always emphasize that everyone should create their own list that helps define their leadership approach and how to articulate that.

It is one thing to have a general leadership point of view. But having a Christ-inspired leadership point of view creates additional challenges. As I developed my leadership approach, I tried to take the time to create my own

Christian leadership philosophy and how and why it is different from, and more expansive from, a purely secular point of view. Throughout my career, I have always been challenged by how I was going to fit my secular leadership approach into my Christian faith (and vice versa) and let my leadership approach align with and stream from my faith.

Tension, of course, creates doubt, and doubt is something that a leader, and perhaps particularly a Christian leader, must face on a regular basis. You are going to doubt your worthiness as a Christian, you are going to doubt whether you are living your life correctly, and you are going to doubt that you did the things you should have been doing. When you are trying to live a Christian life, you are always taking risks. You have a fear that what you are doing will come back and haunt you financially or spiritually. I struggle with that every day. I wonder if I have done enough, I wonder what I should have done in life, and I wonder if I have taken advantage of the opportunities to have greater impact on the lives of others.

We have all had periods in our lives when doubts eat at us. But if you have the mental framework, you can continue to move forward. You can weather the storm. I was talking to one of my executive leaders about this, and she indicated I was great at weathering storms because of my faith. And I think there is some truth to that. Some of it is a maturation process whereby you get more confident in who you are and what you are doing, and you have more security in life. But you are always going to have doubts and bring your requests to God. The philosopher and Lutheran/Protestant theologian Paul Tillich said, "Doubt is an unavoidable part of belief."[1] And that doubt isn't the opposite of faith. It is an element of faith. And that is so true.

The Jefferson Bible as a Metaphor for Our Time

The year 2020 was the two hundredth anniversary of "the Jefferson Bible."[2] The true title of the book is *The Life and Morals of Jesus of Nazareth*, and it is an eighty-four-page version of the New Testament edited and woven together by Thomas Jefferson, our third president of the United States. He edited his version of the Bible through the lens of a Deist and a product of the Enlightenment. As he literally cut and pasted together his version of the New Testament, he left out significant moments in the scripture, including the miracles, the exorcisms, and the resurrection.

As he was working on his version, he wrote to his friend, the former president John Adams, that editing the Gospels was as easy as separating "diamonds from dunghill." In editing the New Testament, Jefferson was careful to say that he was not opposed to the "genuine precepts of Jesus Himself. I am a Christian, but I am a Christian in the only sense in which I believe Jesus wished anyone to be, sincerely attached to His doctrine in preference to all others; ascribing to Him all human excellence."

Some people have criticized the Jefferson Bible, suggesting that if you take out the miracles, Jesus didn't really do much as a leader. The truth is you don't have to have the miracles to determine Jesus's impact on the world. For example, Jesus illustrated tremendous courage at his death, even if you excluded the story of his resurrection.

In fact, at the moment when Thomas is doubting the miracle of the resurrection, the risen Jesus Christ says, "Because you have seen me, you have believed; blessed are those who have not seen and yet have believed" (John 20:29). Christ blesses those who did not have the opportunity to see the resurrection and still believed. For Christ, it was actually at least as important that those who didn't see the miracle became believers. They were perhaps the more blessed because they didn't need to see the miracle to believe.

The miracles can be seen both as a metaphor to help explain a key point and as something that actually happened. As Peter tries to walk on water, his faith fades, and he begins to sink. This story serves not only as an illustration of Christ's power but also as a metaphor about maintaining your faith. When you think of miracles, you need to think beyond the fact that they are merely examples of Christ's power. You need to think about them in the context of what they meant at the time. But let me be clear. I believe the Bible, and I believe in Christ's miracles. That's what God does! But for those who struggle with miracles, taking this approach can still be helpful.

When you look at it, the miracles illustrated Christ's compassion perhaps more than anything. The people he healed were outcasts of society. And he waded into crowds and helped those most in need. If Christ were alive today, he would be in the worst parts of any city or community, wading into the crowds. It demonstrated not only his compassion but who he came to help.

Jefferson took the Bible and created his own perspective. That is exactly what every faith and every individual does. Each era in history has interpreted

Christ's leadership and life in ways that are important to its people. Most of us just don't go about actually cutting and pasting our versions of the New Testament. We all create our own frameworks or purposes (or not) based on what we believe and how we choose to live.

All that said, you have to be careful about creating your own version of the New Testament or Gospels. While we all consciously or unconsciously edit everything, not just the Bible, we have to acknowledge how inexact words can be with multiple interpretations. The danger is that people take scripture out of context and make it their own personal theology. You have to focus on what he did, how he lived his life, as written in the scripture. Not some imagined action of what he would have done. Perhaps that is why Christ chose to speak in parables so often. Consider the parable of the sower as told in the three synoptic Gospels (Matthew 13:1–23; Mark 4:1–20; and Luke 8:4–15).

Jefferson himself probably would have bristled at people referring to his work as "the Jefferson Bible" because he wasn't seeking to create a Bible of his own. He saw the tremendous power of the scripture and of his edited version, saying in an 1812 letter to John Adams: "We must reduce our volume to the simple evangelists, select, even from them, the very words only of Jesus ... there will be found remaining the most sublime and benevolent code of morals which has ever been offered to man."

Versions of Christ

In some ways, it isn't really about the fact that there is no religion, because in many ways, there are many religious opportunities for those who want to find it. But there has been an erosion of what it means to follow a traditional Christian life and the leadership example of Christ.

There have been a number of books published recently talking about how people are inventing their own version of Christ, the Gospels, the New Testament, and the Bible. It feels like we've taken the worship out of worship. For example, in the book *Bad Religion: How We Became a Nation of Heretics*, Ross Gregory Douthat talks about how a growing number of people are inventing their own versions of what Christianity means as they seek ways that religion can stroke their egos and impulses. [3]

As I was reading the book by Kristin Kobes Du Mez called *Jesus and John Wayne: How White Evangelicals Corrupted a Faith and Fractured a Nation*, I found out the author grew up in the same community I did, Sioux Center, Iowa, and went to college at Dordt College, which is literally one house down from where my home was.[4]

In the book, she makes some pretty strong assertions about evangelicals, which I would suggest leads to what I would like to call wide-path leadership (we will define wide-path leadership more fully later in a chapter to follow). She talks about how a segment of white evangelicals have replaced Jesus of the Gospels with a vengeful warrior Christ, and they have used this to rationalize their own beliefs and actions. These evangelicals claim to uphold the Bible as the highest authority in Christian life. While her book may be controversial to some, the point about how we view and project the life of Jesus Christ is critical to what we believe and how we live.

The view that the Bible cannot have errors and is infallible is a tough stand to take, given there are over 31,000 verses in the Bible, written over 1,500 years, in multiple languages, by multiple people, with very different cultural contexts.

This naturally creates considerable tension as you are trying to maintain a narrow path. So you have to look to the example of what Christ did and said to build the foundation for your belief. That is why we focus on the Beatitudes, the Sermon on the Mount, and the Great Commandment (Matthew 22:36–40) as the inspirational center to build on. Because these are things Jesus said and did.

Some churches have made religion academic, debating over points of doctrine. These churches can feel like going to seminary on traditional scripture. Christ didn't live that life. He told basic stories. And other churches focus on feel-good stories and minimize the ministry of Christ. As believers, we sort through churches that tend to be either entirely academic, doctrine focused, or emphasize the emotional experience like positive thinking. You have to always balance what the churches are saying and what helps you grow in your faith.

Creating Their Own Paths

People want to choose the spiritual path that feels right for them—a path that to them is authentic and meaningful. More Americans—and maybe particularly millennials—are creating their own versions of religion and practices, combining the spiritual with other philosophical traditions and metaphysical experiences as they search for meaning and purpose.

Everyone wants to choose. As a lifelong Green Bay Packers fan, I am always interested in what is going on with the team. One time, I happened to hear an interview with Aaron Rodgers, the quarterback of the Packers, where he suggested that religion is way too binary, that religion can be reduced to either it is right or wrong, either A or B.[5] Now, Rodgers is a Stanford graduate, probably the brightest guy in the room, but he oversimplified what Christianity is all about. Christ was not a binary leader. He was more of an and/both leader. There is a great deal of nuance in what Christ taught and in how he led. He supported the laws of God but strongly challenged man-made laws that served only those in power. He considered other perspectives and points of view and met them where they lived. Christ revered the scriptures, but he also sought to convey the deeper meaning to people. He didn't judge people, like the woman in the well, who people stared at and scorned; Christ just told her to sin no more; going forward today, forget the past, live a better life. That is how he lived and led. In this way, the Gospels are both broad based while still focusing on a narrow path.

Some in this country have lost tolerance for what it means to be Christian. Radical views from the Far Left and Far Right all too often have tolerance for only one point of view—theirs.

The thing that always was concerning to me about the former president Trump—and honestly still is concerning—is how he completely obliterated any idea of what might be considered common ground or a common language. Reality became what he said it was at any moment in time. It is the perfect example of how we as a country are creating our own individual realities. We attribute our beliefs and faith to the person we want to support even when it is immensely clear that what the person says and then what he does are completely different. When everyone does that, all you have is chaos. Unfortunately, some people of faith support a particular president's agenda no matter what, because that president can help ensure their agenda to be fulfilled. That is pretty wide-road thinking. When you hold up the leadership example of Christ to many of our former presidents, to any number of other politicians or leaders in any vocation, and you ask yourself, "Do these words and actions line up with what Christ did or would have done?" the immediate answer is absolutely not. These people on either side of the aisle often conduct themselves with little or no grace. And as a Christian, you have to say, "Reject … reject … reject … reject."

Refining the Rules

Sometimes as a Christian, you can feel tension created by people who see themselves as the gatekeepers of Christianity—similar to the Pharisees in Christ's time. And they will use that sense of authority to justify their actions and maintain order as they define it, at all costs. But when you look at the Gospels, Jesus himself was a refiner of rules. In Matthew 5:19, he talks about how he has come not to invalidate the Old Testament but to validate the law. Immediately after that, he takes some of those key Old Testament laws and refines them, saying, "You have heard it said … but I say unto you …" This feels incongruous and creates tension and anxiety.

So what is Christ doing? Can both of these statements be correct? They can be when you consider that Christ may have been suggesting that his disciples should follow the laws of Christ and God, not the laws created by men for their own needs. Or as Peter Enns suggests in his book *The Sin of Certainty: Why God Desires Our Trust More Than Our "Correct" Beliefs,* Christ is encouraging people to follow the heart of the tradition and not necessarily the letter of the faith tradition.[6]

Christ was focused on refining what is right for the person at the right time. When Christ had discussions with the Pharisees and the Sadducees, he went right after them and told them they had used scripture as a power tool and that their positions exploited their roles improperly. And then there were times when he would encourage people to consider their lives and change their actions, but he didn't get into theological discussions. For others, he would challenge their theology. He got into the discussions with the right people at the right time. For example, if someone is new to Christianity, if you get into heavy-duty theological discussions, it can take that person off course. Christ was very refined in how he interacted with people. He was true to the ultimate doctrine and word. But he met people where they were at.

When I grew up, we were drilled on the letter of the law. For some, this can become restrictive and prompt a negative reaction. And for the gatekeepers during the time of Jesus, that became a tool for gaining and maintaining power. They added hundreds of rules to scripture, with no basis to do it other than to keep order and power. Christ supported God's law and refined laws that were man-made and met people where they were at in moving people forward. For me, that framework I learned as a child is incredibly useful as I think about my life today.

Trust versus Absolute Certainty

As a Christian leader, how do you develop a culture of trust versus a culture of absolute certainty? Consider John 3:8, where God's spirit "blows where it chooses, and you hear the sound of it, but you do not know where it comes from."

There are various gatekeepers you meet in life. There are religious gatekeepers who tell you that if you don't do things a certain way, you are not a Christian. You get in leadership circles where if you do things a certain way, you can't be a true leader. There are gatekeepers in social circles. So we face multiple paths as leaders and nonleaders. All of this provides opportunities to find yourself on a broader path.

One thing I have always appreciated is that we were raised with a biblical view of Christianity. It wasn't called that, but it was a certain way of looking at our faith. It gave us a structure. The struggle with that for many is that the structure is too rigid and not where they are at relative to their faith.

There was quote from Sister Joan Chittister, a Benedictine nun, who said, "I do not believe that just because you're opposed to abortion, that that makes you pro-life. In fact, I think in many cases, your morality is deeply lacking if all you want is a child born but not a child fed, not a child educated, not a child housed … Because you don't want any tax money to go there. That's not pro-life. That's pro-birth. We need to have a much broader conversation on what the morality of pro-life is."[7] And that is so true. Some people just look at the single rule and insist on people birthing a child but then won't do anything else to help ensure that baby has an opportunity for a better life. So having the foundation is great, but you have to go beyond having a false certainty that can hamper your ability to get to the truth. And this is where you feel that natural tension between the secular and the sacred.

The Jesus of History and Christ of Faith

Along these same lines, in 1892, the German scholar Martin Kähler made a distinction between the "Jesus of history" and the "Christ of faith." In her book *Freeing Jesus: Rediscovering Jesus as Friend, Teacher, Savior, Lord, Way, and Presence*, Diana Butler Bass talks about how the Jesus of history needed to be recovered, reclaimed, and reinterpreted as the man Jesus who had a radical ministry and life. On the other side of the spectrum, the Christ of faith needed to be renewed, reasserted, and reembraced as the Jesus Christ of orthodox doctrine. She suggests that while some tried to integrate the two, most took sides.[8]

According to Bass, not only do we need to recover, reclaim, and reinterpret Jesus and his ministry, we need to renew our faith, reassert it, and reembrace Christ. I guess I didn't think that people would necessarily take sides about the Jesus of history and the Christ of faith, because to me, it is one and the same.

Looking back on my career, I wish I had had a senior Christian mentor to help me think through my life purpose, how to frame my thoughts, and how to navigate my career. While my upbringing was perhaps a bit out of the ordinary in these contemporary times, we always saw it as an advantage. We had an undergirding of faith—a framework that gave us confidence in our approach to life. But that ups the ante even more for the modern church to help address some of these issues.

Do You Follow the Right Jesus?

There are certain values that tend to lead to a wide path as a Christian leader: we are tempted by the need to be popular, to be successful, to achieve some level of greatness, to avoid suffering or being labeled a failure, or to leave a legacy.

I recently listened to a podcast produced by Ligonier Ministries called *Luther: In Real Time.*[9] It is a reenactment of what happens to the monk Martin Luther after he marches up the steps to the castle church in Wittenberg and nails his ninety-five theses on the door of the church, laying the foundation for the Reformation and the split between the Catholic and Protestant churches. Luther is ordered to recant or face excommunication and death by fire. He was trying to change a church that had lost its way. And when you think about Luther, he was asking the same kind of questions we ask today. Have we taken Christ from the Bible and made him into the current version—the success Jesus? If we look at the concept of servant leadership and how Christ conducted himself, that doesn't always come through in church or through the teaching from modern leaders.

As we all look to balance the tension of the myriad versions of Christ that are available to us, it might be helpful to ask some of the same questions Luther asked. Have we molded Christ in a certain way to meet our society's view of him? Or our own? We need to see Christ as he lived, not based on modern interpretations. In society right now, we like to erase some hard edges. We need to look at Christ as he is in the Gospels and not a dumbed-down version.

There Is Memorizing Text, the Gospel according to Me … and Then There Is Truth

A famous verse in John (8:31–32) talks about finding and knowing the truth: "To the Jews who had believed him, Jesus said, 'If you hold to my teaching, you are really my disciples. Then you will know the truth, and the truth will set you free.'"

It is important to start from the perspective that you want to use the Bible and scripture as it is intended to be used and not as it is convenient for you to use. There are too many examples of people using Bible verses out of context and not based on what Christ actually did. We all do it at times. Understanding the historical context is important. You can memorize Bible verses, and you can understand historical context, which will help you get to the truth to some degree, but there is more.

How do you find the truth when on the one hand you find those who rigidly and evangelically interpret the Bible, and those who are on the other side of the spectrum who say it is "the Word according to me"? When you think about it, people on both ends of this spectrum are actually pretty closely aligned in that they both believe their version to be the correct one and are unwilling to accept any other ideas. Both of these extremes can create a crisis of faith.

We need to have a healthy acceptance that we are all flawed, and as a result, our interpretation of scripture may be flawed also. And we have to understand that the Bible is a collection of Gospels and writings that were created over centuries by humans with varying points of view and in the context of their own contemporary environment. How do you find and know the truth? First, we can recognize the diversity of the scripture and acknowledge that it can lead to an even deeper understanding of what Christ did and how that applies to us today. As Christ-inspired leaders, our points of reference should include not only scripture and historical context but also reason, experience, and, most importantly, the guidance of the Holy Spirit.

Rationalizing to Fit Christ Where We Want Him to Fit

A.W. Tozer was an American Christian pastor, author, magazine editor, and spiritual mentor. He died in 1963, but his writing has remained influential in the Christian and Evangelical world even today. In 2000, his book *The Pursuit of God* was named to Christianity Today's list of 100 Books of the Century. A new book, *Lead Like Christ: Reflecting the Qualities and Character of Christ in Your Ministry*, was published in July 2021. His writing is very passionate, perhaps a bit too much for some, but what he says has been useful to me over the years, including a blog series on Bible Gateway called *Tozer on Leadership*.[10]

One of his blog posts talks about deadly rationalism, and today there is a radical evangelical rationalism not unlike the rationalism taught by the scribes and Pharisees. The Pharisees took the Christian faith and added hundreds of rules. When you add things to what Christ did, and we make that the new Christian standard, then we change the model to be more modern, more contemporary, and less clear. The model morphs into the success Gospel that if you pray for it, God has a wonderful plan for your life. Sadly, God may not have a wonderful plan for our lives. That is hard to think about. That leads to our rationalizing to gloss over the challenges we face in life.

During the Civil War, people on both sides of the slavery issue quoted scripture to rationalize their actions. We see the same thing today. We rationalize everything we do. We rationalize our lives away. People rationalize when they take advantage of companies or organizations, which is true of religious organizations as much as it is of Wall Street barons. People will say they deserve it, they are a special case, they are above the fray. But no one is above the fray.

You can easily talk yourself into doing certain things. As a major corporation, the organization I lead is at times scrutinized by the news media. That is their job, and we all understand that. All we ask is that there is fairness in the coverage. Many times, our organization has been unhappy with what we perceived as unfair coverage by news organizations. Credible news organizations try to keep the news side and the opinion side of their publications separate. Sometimes the different sides of the media don't agree with each other. And when we had an occasion to meet with both the editorial and news sides of the organization on a particular story or stories they published and we disagreed with, the news and editorial sections both have their views of reality, and neither is quite right. But that is what we do in life every day. Rationalize our choices rather than look to the example of Christ for direction.

Sometimes it seems like we are always trying to fit Jesus into what we want. It is like we have this spiritual whiteboard, and on it we put those things we really want God to make happen. When, of course, we have things in reverse. We should be asking God how to fulfill His plan, not our personal list, not our personal spiritual whiteboard. That is a constant challenge for everyone: "This is what I want to do, so, God, here it is. Please bless my plan!"

It is through our faith and the guidance of the Holy Spirit that we can find truth and avoid faulty rationalization. We will talk more about how God's wisdom will be revealed by the Holy Spirit in the chapter on finding perspective, but the need to look to the Holy Spirit for guidance is spelled out in 1 Corinthians 2:14: "The person without the Spirit does not accept the things that come from the spirit of God, but considers them foolishness and cannot understand them because they are discerned only through the spirit." My understanding and appreciation of the Holy Spirit is greater today than ever in my life. I just wish I had this appreciation thirty years ago. It would have made life a lot more stress-free.

Dean Martin and Projecting to Christian Leadership

When I was a kid, I often watched the Dean Martin variety show with my parents, which featured beautiful women called the Golddiggers. My mom loved Dean Martin. She would often say that Dean Martin was a good man and a good Christian. And my dad would say, "What are you talking about?

Dean Martin smokes, he always has a drink with him on the show, and he is dancing with all those women. Are you kidding me? How could this person be a good Christian?" And then my mom would say something like, "But I can tell he has a good heart." It is hard to fathom exactly how my mom decided he had a good heart, yet she did. It is humorous to remember that this exchange between my parents happened often. Now he may have been a good Christian person, but from the standpoint of someone with a strong Dutch reformation background, it strained, let's say, credibility. But this illustrates the point that sometimes we make people out to be what they may or may not be. In the same way, as Christians, some have set out to make this country their vision of what Christianity means, and as a result, they have created a version of Christianity that doesn't necessarily relate to the leadership example of Christ.

We certainly have had our share of wide-path, high-ranking political figures, business leaders, pastors, celebrities, and other high-profile individuals who talk a good game and portray themselves to be very religious but turn out to do the exact opposite of what Christ did. We all sin and make mistakes, and sometimes television projects attributes on to those we admire—like my mom did with Dean Martin.

In working through the tension you feel as a result of this daily conflict, you have to think about who you are and where you are going in order to find your strength. If you rely on work as your only source of strength, and your life is wrapped up in the leadership at work, you may struggle to find that strength. It may be more meaningful if you think about how you get up every day and apply a servant leadership approach and the principles of Christ.

Early in my career, I thought my purpose was to do a good job, make sure we had the resources to help our patients, and things of that nature. And now my purpose in life is to honor God, lead with Christ's example, and use the opportunities I have to help others. That is a hard concept to understand when you are twenty-five. You work through it and work toward it as you gain wisdom. And at points in life, you are more vocal about your Christian faith than at others. And at times, you wish you could go back in time and change things—how you thought and acted, what you said. But that is how we change and mature in life.

T W O

INTEGRATING SCIENCE AND SCRIPTURE

Having spent the majority of my career in health care, and the majority of that time in a non-faith-based organization, there have been some natural ethical and moral questions creating tension between my faith as a Christian and the science-based nature of health care and how we provide care. Many Christians, including members of both political parties, have strong views about multiple causes, including reproductive rights, gay rights, and things like stem cell research. That leads to moments of tension virtually every day, where there is a need to balance religious beliefs and the framework of the Gospels with the practicality of leading an organization.

One of the most controversial issues I dealt with in my career is related to abortion services in the communities where my organization was providing health care services. In one particular community, there was one independent organization that provided abortions in a metro area. The state was changing its policy related to requiring transfer agreements related to abortion patients. Transfer agreements allow independent health care organizations to transfer patients to a hospital if there is a medical need. These agreements were required by the state, and no facility could perform abortions if they did not have a transfer agreement. Some would argue these are clinically necessary, and others would say these decisions are politically motivated.

While we did not have an official transfer agreement with this abortion clinic, we did, and always have had, an overarching policy (as do most health care organizations) that states that we will care for any patient in clinical need. Because of this, we would accept any abortion patient in need of care.

Historically, a state-owned hospital had a transfer agreement, but when the state passed a law prohibiting such agreements with state-owned hospitals, it quickly became an issue for others. The pro-life contingent was demanding that we not sign any transfer agreement, citing it was our mission to do this. The pro-choice contingent demanded we sign a transfer agreement, also saying that it was our mission to do so.

The issue of whether or not our facilities would sign a transfer agreement to accept abortion patients was ultimately decided by our board of directors. I was criticized for not stopping it, as if I had authority to do so. But as a community-based organization, the community represented by our board members was the body that was ultimately responsible for making the decision. After a comprehensive and passion-filled debate, we put it to a confidential vote, with a majority deciding the outcome. To ensure impartiality, only two people knew the results of the vote—our general counsel and the person who helped count the votes. To this day, I do not know which way the members of the board voted. But as a group, the board voted to sign the transfer agreement and for our organization to formalize the organization's decision to accept transfers when medically necessary. That was an extremely tough issue, and the board did a remarkable job in thoughtfully considering all perspectives. The decision, of course, generated significant positive and negative responses, and many of the negative comments directed toward me came from Christians.

It was tough for me because in my heart of hearts, I don't believe abortion is ever right unless a mother's life is at risk. But I also don't believe we can judge others in these situations, which is not the opinion of many Christians. We were a community/mission-based organization, and we had to reflect the views of the community we served. It wasn't about me. I didn't and don't own the organization. It was about the community. It was not, and is not, my place to judge. We take care of everyone, whatever the need. And caring for everyone is based in servant leadership and, to me, an essential Christian concept. One of the concerns I have had as a Christian is that often we judge other people in how they live but then do little or nothing to help these people find opportunities to change their lives.

According to a recent report by the Pew Research Center, the most common answer to the question about whether or not abortion should be legal remains "it depends."[1] That said, three-quarters of white evangelicals say that abortion should be illegal. Eighty-one percent of white evangelicals see abortion as morally wrong, compared to 46 percent of Americans overall.

For many, there is no right answer. You start to rationalize and judge people. And in our judgment, we lose all aspect of Christ's love. People get locked in, not just Christians.

As a leader, when you disagree with an organizational decision over ethical or moral issues, you have a choice: you can accept the decision or you can leave the organization. Or you can consider Christ's leadership example to look past differences and continue to make an impact in the community you have with the resources at your disposal. This is where many will criticize and condemn such thinking and point out the absolute correctness of their view.

We all sin. We have lists of them. Some cheat on their taxes; some cheat on their significant others; some mistreat their children and their employees. There are thousands of examples. It is for God to judge and determine whether or not you are allowed into heaven. In the interchange with the Samaritan woman, Christ tells her in no uncertain terms to knock it off. Don't do that stuff anymore. Stop. And sin no more. That's true for her situation, and it is true for us all. Stop and sin no more. And move on. That's what we all should focus on every day.

How Assertive Should You Be in Your Faith?

Throughout my career, like many Christians, I have always struggled with the concept of being a Christian leader in a non-faith-based organization. Some people would say I should be more assertive about my faith in the work environment. I have never felt it was my place to overtly do that. Most health care organizations are community/mission-based, and I always felt I had to be somewhat careful in interjecting my personal views, including my view of faith. It is different when you actually own the company. I have always believed that, by my example, people would see my faith and understand it without me having to explicitly spell it out. For me, leading by example was the way to create a faith-based approach throughout the organization and in the communities we serve. I understand for some that is not enough. It is part of the narrow path that for me still gets a little confusing. It is easy to tell someone what to do, but it is not as easy when it is you making decisions.

The question you ask is whether it is important to bring all people along, which means engaging people of all faiths, ethnicities, political views, and sexual orientation, listening to all points of view.

Science and Sacred Can Interact Together

While it is true that many natural tensions exist between the world of science and the sacred, it is possible, and even necessary, to connect and integrate the two worlds.

Francis S. Collins is someone steeped in science and the secular. He recently retired as the director of the National Institutes of Health and is a physician-geneticist who discovered the genes associated with a number of diseases and led the Human Genome Project. He is also a recent recipient of the Templeton Prize, which celebrates scientific and spiritual curiosity, and he is the author of the book *The Language of God: A Scientist Presents Evidence for Belief*.[2] He writes in his book that, as a scientist, a belief in God is not only rational, but the principles of faith are complementary with the principles of science. He wholeheartedly believes that the scientific and the spiritual can and should be integrated. In the book, he suggested that science helps us understand the natural world, but that questions like "What is the meaning of human existence?" and "Why did the universe come into being?" are more suited for the realm of the sacred. We shouldn't be forced to choose between the sacred and the scientific. When people are heavily on either side of this spectrum—all science or all sacred—it is very easy to be confused and disillusioned, which can lead to a crisis in faith.

We are going to discuss this more in the chapter on life purpose, but the organization I work for is partnering with an international behavior design company, and one part of what they are doing is conducting a comprehensive national survey related to purpose and fulfillment. It turns out that having a purpose creates a resiliency, and as result, you are less prone to depression and anxiety. If you have a strong sense of purpose, you can better address some of the societal factors like poverty, education, and housing that so impact our health and well-being. It is also a predictor of engagement. Faith is important to a sense of life purpose. When you think about combining the science of health and well-being and the purpose in emulating Christ, it can be pretty powerful.

Health care is really driven by science, so there are natural tensions that arise when making decisions about caring for patients and about new and innovative ways to improve health care outcomes. Some of the most innovative things involve the use of technologies that are not necessarily accepted by organized religion. For example, we had a decision to make related to working with a company that used stem cells in the treatment of traumatic brain injury and possibly Alzheimer's disease. The project showed great promise, but these stem cell therapies also included some risk, and in some cases these treatments were (and still are not) not available in the United States because of the ethical debate over using stem cells. This tension raised questions about the source of the stem cells and the opportunity to let others know that treatment options were available. After doing our due diligence and carefully and thoughtfully evaluating this issue, we decided to move forward. So we evaluate each project separately and then test that against faith.

Have We Cheapened the Meaning of Miracle?

In some ways, we have cheapened what a miracle is and what it means. Today, everything is a miracle. Miracle drugs. Miracle workouts. Miracle diets. Miracle cures. We compare secular accomplishments with spiritual miracles. We water down the biblical to make it more secular. Some accept our political leaders as miraculous, when the reverse is true. Or that the pandemic is really a plague because we didn't honor God. True miracles cannot be explained by the laws of nature; they are by definition supernatural.

That doesn't mean the secular must exclude the miraculous. As Francis Collins explains in his book, it just means that there is a need to admit that there is something that might exist outside of nature, and when we do that, then for the scientist, miracles can and do occur.[3]

That might be hard for researchers or scientists because there is no hard proof for certain things. Consider the book *Evidence That Demands a Verdict* by Josh McDowell.[4] He was an atheist who went out to prove that Christianity was false. As he conducted his research, he would cross reference historic materials at different periods of time to fact check evidence to validate or negate whether things actually happened. He found that there are thousands of sources that reaffirm what is in the Bible. Yet scientists may have a hard time believing because they feel the evidence is faith based.

During his brief ministry, Christ spent a lot of time completing miracles, such as healing the sick, freeing the demon-possessed, raising people from the dead, calming storms, walking on water, creating massive fish catches, turning water into wine, and multiplying food to feed massive crowds. Indeed, "the blind receive their sight, the lame walk, the lepers are cleansed, the deaf hear, the dead are raised, and the poor have good news brought to them" (Matthew 11:2–6). So, of course, we all naturally wonder, what kind of man is this? And how should we think of miracles?

Francis Collins echoes the philosophy of C. S. Lewis in that miracles disrupt natural law.

That is exactly what Christ did. He created conditions that disrupted nature and weren't logical when he raised people from the dead and performed other miraculous events. He disrupted the senses.

You can't count on miracles in your life. But when you think about what disrupts you when things happen, do they serve as a miracle? There is this great cartoon showing this scientist with an intricate, elegant mathematical formula on a whiteboard, and then a cloud extends from it that says, "And then a miracle happens."[5] That is a little like what C. S. Lewis and Francis Collins are saying. There is something that causes the need for a miracle, and there is an outcome.

Not Miracles but Signs: A Way to Think about Miracles for Nonbelievers

If you are struggling with the idea of miracles, perhaps you need to look no further than the Gospel according to John for help. In the Gospel according to John, he doesn't really talk about miracles. Plus, there is an absence of exorcisms. Instead, he calls things that were described as miracles in other Gospels "signs." The transformation of water into wine is the first of Jesus's signs in John; the second sign is the healing of an official's son. And in John 20:30–31, he says, "Jesus performed many other signs in the presence of his disciples, which are not recorded in this book. But these are written that you may believe that Jesus is the Messiah, the Son of God, and that by believing you may have life in his name." John replaces the word *miracles* with the word *signs* throughout his Gospel. And like the miracles, these signs result in outcomes that lead people to true faith.

So the concept of signs and miracles can be synonymous. Christ did say he would perform miracles as signs so that people would believe. He also said blessed are those who believe and didn't see these miracles. The signs pointed people to God.

The idea of miracles can turn people off. We had some friends who took their son to church, and the sermon was about Jonah and the whale, and the son said, "This is the silliest thing I have ever heard," and never went back. So if you can coach the idea of miracles as signs, not to minimize the importance of miracles but to bring people from a place where they are at in time, that can be effective.

From a leadership perspective, personally, I see more and more signs that Christ was the greatest leader ever. It continues to reinforce who Christ was and what his leadership style was. These signs or miracles can help point us to this Christ-inspired leadership style. Some Christians might not want me to say this, but it may not be as important that you believe in miracles. As a Christian, it is critically important to consider Christ as my savior. For others, what might be more important, though, is to consider those signs in your life you can point to where you can see Christ's example in your life and as a leader.

Secular and biblical views can coexist. But to elevate the secular to the point where nothing exists beyond what we can see is shortsighted.

In this book, you will read about a number of secular articles and books that influenced me as a Christian leader. For me, I embrace the science and look at it through a Christian lens, and the combined perspective has helped make me a better leader. Using a Christ-inspired approach to leadership has made a significant difference for me. Would Christ fire the bottom 10 percent of the workforce, as some secular leadership gurus have suggested? No. Was Christ the father of leading change and servant leadership? Absolutely. Leading change—it's in the Bible. Servant leadership—it's in the Bible. Emotional intelligence—it is in the Bible. Storytelling—it's in the Bible. Resiliency—it's in the Bible. Purpose—are you kidding me? Christ was all purpose. Taking this view reaffirms my leadership approach. It is a way to construct our worldview as a tool in making everyday decisions. It is like navigating your way up the mountain toward being a successful leader, and at the top, you find Jesus.

THREE

SAYING YOU ARE A CHRISTIAN LEADER AND BEING A CHRISTIAN LEADER MAY NOT BE THE SAME THING

In his book *Jesus through the Centuries*, Jaroslav Pelikan presents a survey of Christ's place in history and his impact on culture during different eras.[1] At different points in history, Jesus has served as a kind of Cosmic Christ, the Teacher of Common Sense, the Poet of the Spirit, the Liberator, the Man Who Belongs to the World, and our Lord and Savior, just to name a few.

All of these descriptors are completely accurate when thinking about Christ. However, there is one term you don't see as a chapter title for this book: Christ as a leader, much less the greatest leader that ever lived. Perhaps it is inferred in the titles, but it is never explicitly stated. Perhaps that should be a starting point when considering the role Christ played throughout history, rather than something understood but not stated. In three short years, Jesus Christ completely (and radically) changed the world for all time and had an impact that is often hard to appreciate and comprehend.

The Gospels are essential when understanding Christ's role, because they describe what Christ did during his ministry. As people read the Gospels, many will immediately see Christ as the great teacher. And that is so true! But in some ways, the idea of teacher and leader are synonymous. The Christ of the Gospels not only provides great wisdom, but through his example and his actions as well as his words, he exemplifies the perfect example of leadership. In fact, as we will see throughout this book, the narrative in the Gospels anticipates many successful leadership books of contemporary times. When you think about how Christ exemplified the

Beatitudes and lived the Sermon on the Mount, you begin to think of him as the greatest leader of all time.

Of course, focusing on Christ as leader is in some way a bit of a disservice to who Christ is. At the core of Christianity, we believe he came to save us from our sins, yet his leadership examples can't be ignored. In some cases, contemporary church leaders have ignored or minimized his leadership example, and in some circumstances, they have tried to supplant themselves and secular leader types as the leadership example rather than Christ, which in turn has damaged the church's credibility and created false and destructive narratives. This makes the church less relevant to those who are seeking how to understand and rationalize their religious and personal lives. Personally, an earlier focus on Christ as the best example of how Christians (and everyone, really) should lead would have been extremely helpful to me as I modeled my personal approach to leadership.

With this in mind, we wanted to test the theory of Christ as leader, so we worked with the research firm Great Lakes Marketing to conduct a national online survey of business leaders. It is a small sample size consisting of 120 respondents in leadership positions from middle management to owners of companies, but the survey provides some interesting directional insights that could inspire more detailed research on the subject. We wanted to test some areas we knew we were going to cover in this book, including leading change, servant leadership, purpose, and perspective. What follows is a brief summary of the results.

What you start to see as you look at the survey results is a definition of what it means to be a Christian leader in a secular world in this country. Some of the results probably will confirm some thoughts you have had about Christian leadership. Others, I think, might surprise you.

Defining a "Christian Leader"

About half of the respondents were categorized as Christian leaders because they live intentionally with Christ as a leadership example and faith plays a strong role in their leadership style. Respondents who believe faith plays a strong role in their leadership style are influenced by prayer, the Bible's teachings, and leadership figures. They tend to align workplace or leadership duties and personal religious beliefs.

Christian leaders tend to

- admire religious leaders;
- refer to their religious beliefs in a time of crisis at work or in life;
- always or sometimes spend time in prayer before making business decisions and consider Christian values in decision-making. In comparison, those not identifying as Christian leaders indicated they rarely or never considered Christian values in decision-making;
- believe faith plays a strong role in their life purpose. Ninety-three percent indicated they were able to define their life purpose, compared to 65 percent of those who did not identify as a Christian leader;
- feel that businesses should use faith-based strategies; and
- experience situations in the workplace where their religious beliefs conflict with the organization's decisions.

Interestingly, 59 percent of those considering themselves Christian leaders indicated that someone could be considered a Christian leader even if they didn't regularly attend religious services.

Living Intentionally with Christ as a Leadership Example

Of those surveyed, 75 percent said they lived intentionally with Christ as an example of leadership. These people indicated they use prayer and Bible study to help guide their business decisions and during times of crisis. They also agree that businesses should use faith-based strategies and mentor others to use Judeo-Christian values in the workplace. They are also more likely to:

- always or sometimes rely on teachings from the Bible to influence their leadership decisions
- think of Christ as both a teacher and a leader
- believe they work for Christian-oriented or Christian-influenced organizations
- be middle-aged and male

Top Three Leaders of All Time

One of the most startling results of the survey related to a question asking respondents to name the top three religious leaders they have admired in their lives. Those who did not identify as Christian leaders, as you might expect, identified Christ as one of the top three leaders just 12 percent of the time.

More significantly, *only 13 percent of those identifying as Christian leaders identified Jesus Christ as one of those top three leaders.*

That is a pretty stunning statistic. Stated another way, nearly nine of ten people identifying as a Christian leader *did not* list Christ as one of their top three leaders.

Wow! Maybe we should stop here! That is why this book is needed!

To those who identified as a Christian leader but who did not identify Christ as a top leader, we asked a follow-up question: "Why didn't you think of Christ as one of your admired leaders?" We received some interesting rationalizations. The responses fell into three general categories: 1) assumed he was ineligible/not alive; 2) he is too special for this description; or 3) I don't know. A couple of respondents recognized they had made a mistake and indicated they should have listed Christ as a top-three leader.

Instead of selecting Christ as a leader, 43 percent selected other religious leaders—for example, national and international religious leaders, pastors of regionally and nationally recognized megachurches, and local pastors. So you begin to understand the concept of the impact of Christian leaders and organizations pointing to secular leaders as the example for how we should live.

This is indeed the crux of this book! We may think of Christ as a teacher, or as a cosmic Christ, or a man for the world, but for whatever reason, as a country, when we think about leadership, we don't make the connection of Christ as a leader. And that is a shame, because there is so much to learn from his leadership example.

Christian Leaders Don't Necessarily See Themselves as Servant Leaders

For me, Christ is *the* example of servant leadership. One of the chapters later in this book will focus on servant leadership. You might think that Christian leaders would identify themselves as servant leaders. But in our survey, only

43 percent of those identifying as Christian leaders considered themselves to be servant leaders; 52 percent considered themselves to be traditional leaders.

Looking at the leadership example of Christ, there appears to be a significant disconnection in following the leadership example of Christ.

Of those who did not identify as a Christian leader, the percent of identifying as a servant leader was even lower. Only 21 percent thought of themselves as a servant leader; 52 percent considered themselves more traditional leaders; and 27 percent said they weren't sure. That's pretty astounding!

Those who identified as servant leaders admire religious leaders and reflect that admiration in their leadership decisions. That said, only 16 percent of those who identified as a servant leader identified Jesus Christ as one of their top three leaders.

Perhaps this is something that requires more in-depth research, because these are pretty striking results. There seem to be some significant disconnects among Christians and how they view Christ as a leader and his approach to leadership. Instead of having Christ front and center in leadership thinking, Christ is largely ignored or very much on the periphery. If Christ is not the example, then who is?

Compared to traditional leaders, those who describe their leadership style as "servant" are more likely to

- admire religious leaders,
- think of Christ as both a teacher and a leader,
- say faith plays a strong role in their leadership style, and
- agree that businesses should use faith-based strategies.

Compared to servant leaders, those who describe their leadership style as traditional are more likely to

- say faith plays a moderate to neutral role in their leadership style,
- neither agree nor disagree that businesses should use faith-based strategies, and
- be younger and male.

Age and Christian Leadership

Younger respondents (in their twenties and thirties) tended to guide their decisions and leadership style using religious beliefs. That said, they are more often self-described as traditional leaders rather than servant leaders. They use their religious beliefs to help guide their decisions and leadership style.

In contrast, older respondents (ages sixty and over) are less likely to define their life purpose and business life using religious belief. This might seem counterintuitive, because you might think that as you get older, you would have a clearer idea of your life purpose and a stronger sense of faith.

Middle Managers Make a Stronger Connection to Work and Faith than Top Levels of Organizational Leadership

In the survey, we asked leaders to categorize themselves either as middle managers, upper management, or as presidents/owners of companies.

Based on the findings from the survey, middle managers are more inclined to refer to religious beliefs in the workplace and experience conflicts between their beliefs and organizational decisions than other management levels. Sixty-three percent of middle managers indicated they had made business decisions that ignored their spiritual beliefs. This is the gap that happens between Sunday services and Monday morning.

Owners/presidents were far less likely to say they have had situations in the workplace where their religious beliefs were in conflict with organizational decisions. Seventy-seven percent of owners/presidents surveyed indicated that they had not made a business decision that ignored their spiritual beliefs.

Upper management fell in the middle between owners/presidents and middle managers related to experiencing conflicts between their beliefs and organizational decisions. Compared to owners/presidents, upper management is also more likely to admire professional mentors as leaders and is able to define their life purpose.

African American Leaders More Likely to Align Faith and Workplace

The survey asked respondents to identify as white/Caucasian, African America, Asian, Hispanic, or other (or declined to answer).

African Americans are more likely to fall into the "Christian leader" category and tend to align their religious beliefs with workplace and leadership duties. However, only a small percentage of African Americans listed Jesus Christ as one of their top three religious leaders.

Compared to Caucasians, African Americans and Hispanics are more likely to

- always or sometimes spend time in prayer before making business decisions,
- always or sometimes rely on teachings from the Bible to influence their leadership decisions,
- live intentionally with Christ as an example of leadership,
- say faith plays a strong role in their life purpose and leadership style,
- agree that businesses should use faith-based strategies, and
- have made business decisions that ignored spiritual beliefs.

Owners/Presidents Less Likely to Experience Work/Faith Conflicts

Young respondents are more likely to experience conflicts between their religious beliefs and workplace decisions. Respondents who have experienced workplace and religious belief conflict often use their religious values to make business and leadership decisions. Because owners make many key decisions in an organization, they naturally have greater opportunity to create situations creating conflict. That said, findings from the survey indicated that owners/presidents of companies were less likely to have experienced work/faith conflicts. Those leaders who have not experienced work/faith conflicts are more likely to be not sure of their leadership style compared to those who have experienced these conflicts.

Compared to leaders who have not experienced work and religious belief conflicts, those who have experienced conflicts between work and their religious beliefs are more likely to

- admire professional mentors, religious leaders, personal mentors, political leaders, and leaders within their company or industry,
- refer to their religious beliefs in a time of crisis at work or in life,
- always or sometimes spend time in prayer before making business decisions,
- always or sometimes rely on teachings from the Bible to influence their leadership decisions,
- say faith plays a strong role in their life purpose and leadership style,
- agree that businesses should use faith-based strategies,
- have made a business decision that ignored their spiritual beliefs, and
- always or sometimes recommend using Christian values to make business decisions.

Questions and Considerations

For me, there were two critical takeaways from this survey.

1. Only 13 percent of those identifying as Christian leaders identified Jesus Christ as one of those top three leaders.
2. Only 43 percent of those identifying as Christian leaders considered themselves to be servant leaders; 52 percent considered themselves to be traditional leaders.

We need to take a deeper look at why Christian leaders aren't identifying more with the leadership example of Christ. Is it an educational issue? A broader cultural issue? Have we created "sometime" Christian leaders because we have so undervalued its importance?

The same questions could be asked related to why Christian leaders don't see themselves as servant leaders. Why don't more presidents/owners of organizations consider Christ's leadership example when resolving conflicts? The survey creates additional questions for more research. But it does provide a sense of how some perceive what Christian leadership is—and isn't.

And the simple, stunning fact that only 13 percent of Christian leaders identified Christ as a top leader is indication enough for the necessity of this book. The question then is, if Christ is not the leadership example you follow, then who? Secular leaders? The leaders the world has deemed successful? It would seem that if churches emphasized Jesus Christ as the greatest leader ever, then more professionals would point to his example as how to lead.

In this chapter, we talked about how some people who identify as Christian leaders do not necessary act like Christ-inspired leaders. In the next chapter, we talk about leaders and organizations who have gone the slippery slope to wide-path leaders, with disastrous result.

F O U R

THE SLIPPERY SLOPE TO WIDE-PATH LEADERSHIP

You don't have to look hard to find an example of failed Christian leaders. The recent Southern Baptist Convention scandal is just one example. These are leaders, and by extension their organizations, who preach the narrow path of Christ's example but in reality are what many would call wide-path leaders.

How do you define a wide-path leader? Matthew 23:3–30, which includes the "Woe to you" list, captures nicely the negative attributes of the Pharisees, which in turn serves as an effective description of the characteristics of a wide-path leader. These leaders

- say one thing but do another,
- put heavy burdens on the people but none on themselves,
- are very overt and public in how they display their religion, including prayer,
- make converts who end up being worse off than before converting,
- are poor spiritual guides,
- use a double standard to justify their actions,
- look nice on the outside but are corrupt on the inside,
- make a big deal out of smaller offenses but commit significant offenses themselves,
- seem to be spiritually alive, but inside they are withered, and
- create beautiful monuments but are bankrupt spiritually.

Wide-path leaders are also self-righteous, which Jesus vividly illustrates in the parable of the Pharisee and the tax collector in Luke 18:9–14. One exemplifies the Roman culture; the other represents a more Christian culture. As the two go to the temple to pray, the Pharisee represents the empire, while the tax collector resists Roman occupation and law. One embraces the culture; the other rejects it. As they pray, the Pharisee is prideful; the tax collector pleads for mercy. Their words reveal their hearts. "The mouth speaks what the heart is full of" (Luke 6:45).

I don't think it is a stretch to say that we all know leaders like this.

We help create wide-path leaders when we do the following:

- hold out secular leaders from all professions who express ideas opposite of the Beatitudes and Sermon on the Mount as examples of Christian leadership versus focusing on the leadership example of Christ
- project our beliefs to make wide-path leaders what we believe they should be, not based on the historic context of the Gospels / New Testament
- rationalize concepts and ideas from the Gospels / New Testament to create a version of the leadership example of Christ "according to me"
- help them see themselves as personal gatekeepers of the law, like the Pharisees, and work at all costs to maintain that authority
- enable them to see themselves as becoming greater in importance as Christ becomes smaller, versus Christ becoming greater and the individual becoming smaller

And by extension, we can define wide-path churches and organizations as those that

- are more concerned about ensuring their existence rather than the cross. They are corporatized entities that focus on numbers as their main measure of success;
- follow political leaders in our country who have led shaky ethical and moral lives and are held up by some Christians as examples of Christian leaders because they provide transactional power to a position taken by the church and their members; and
- are solely focused on numbers, consumer experiences, and not on the meaning of Christ's example.

What follows are some examples of how churches and individuals, either intentionally or unintentionally, illustrate the concept of what it means to be a wide-path leader and organization.

We Worship the Wrong Things and People

The professional football player Tom Brady is really an iconic figure in our country. Widely recognized as the greatest quarterback of all time, he is a seven-time Super Bowl champion, five-time Super Bowl MVP, and three-time league most valuable player. In many, many ways, he is an example for all of us. That said, I have some notes from old interviews with Tom on *60 Minutes* and other programs where he wasn't sure what the meaning of life was. Fast-forward, and now there is this new idea of achieving perfection, having the perfect human body with a perfect diet and exercise program to enable him to play football at a high level well beyond what is considered a normal career length. All this is great, and he has had a remarkable career, but it gives a false impression of what our life goals should be. It is the idea of the individual physical pursuit of perfection versus the pursuit of a Christ-inspired life. The reward for a Christian is more about how you are going to live your life in service of others, in pursuit of preaching the Gospel and preaching and illustrating Christian values, not being focused on yourself. And then you see this example of an individual who is glorified for striving to create this perfect athlete. He may be among the greatest of all time as an athlete, but we shouldn't worship people like that; we should be following the example of the inner-city pastor who gets up every day and feeds inner-city kids who don't know where their next meal is coming from. I don't know Tom Brady's faith, but I can only hope his commitment to football in some way matches his spiritual goals.

Christ did not hang around with the cream of the crop. He hung around in small towns. He didn't go to the New York of the day. He didn't go to the major meccas, like Rome. He didn't hang with the religious leaders of the day, politicians, athletes, celebrities, academics, or successful business types. He didn't hang out at any social club. His disciples were a rogues' gallery, and he associated with the "undesirables" of his day. He grew up in a small town and lived off the grid. There is a point there: be careful about who you follow and associate with. Oftentimes, what people are selling is not what Christ told us to do or how he lived.

Militant Christians

In a blog post, A. W. Tozer talks about how fanatical Christians make other Christians unwilling to profess their faith and turn away from prayer, scripture, and the Holy Spirit, ultimately leading people away from a narrow path and down a more secular road.[1]

Some people are militant in their faith. Christ was militant with people who took religion and added their laws and rules for their own advantage. He wasn't militant toward people who were struggling with life and their faith. He was gracious to people who were considered lowly during his time. He recognized women, the poor, the sick, the disabled, and those struggling with mental health issues.

Militant leaders wind up alienating people rather than bringing them to their cause. For example, some, not all, on the radical right can be fanatical and will criticize you for not standing up for their version of faith. In the same way, some people on the radical left will preach about tolerance, but they can be some of the most intolerant people you will find if you disagree with their point of view. People on either edge are not going to be good examples of Christian faith.

Sadly, Pastors in the News

Unfortunately, pastors across the country have been in the news for all the wrong reasons, in ways that make them examples of wide-path leaders and leadership. On his Instagram account, Ben Kirby identifies pastors who are wearing expensive sneakers.[2] There is another story of a famous evangelical pastor, Rev. Rick Joyner, whose kids have told him to pipe down. We could list a number of religious leaders (along with every other profession) who have failed, but the point is not to judge them but to think about what lesson we should learn from that behavior.

When we see church leaders falter like this, increasingly, the narrow gate that leads to eternal light seems harder to attain. Some Christian leaders will fail, and some people live to point out their sins. When you think about the title of this book, you can imagine a person walking toward two paths, one a broad, lush path, and then off to the side, there is a much smaller, more challenging, narrow path. And that is symbolic of the decisions Christians make.

John the Baptist said to Jesus, "You must become greater, I must become less" (John 3:30). That is advice we should take. We constantly need to be less and allow Christ to become greater in our lives. In this wide-path form of leadership, the individual is greater, and Christ is minimized.

Pastors, as fallible human beings just like the rest of us, fall into that trap. They get accolades. They take it all in. And somehow, some of them rationalize wearing thousand-dollar sneakers, flying in private jets, and basically begging for money.

I saw a little devotional on Instagram. On this post, there was a person talking about how we as Christians look at God as a historic figure and that we trust God until we don't trust in him. And we think, *We trust God, but if he isn't getting the job done, we will take over.* And when we take over, we take the secular route. My fear is that if we don't have a more Christ-centered world view, then we are going to be prone to drift. And it is far too easy to drift.

In my experience, this is where church has failed, because they haven't done enough to make the connection between church, work life, and life in general. Christ did! I have been fortunate recently to have two pastors who have really been able to provide examples that connect to what I do every day. And that has helped in day-by-day struggles to have a clearer pathway.

What Interests You More, Who Jesus Is or What He Can Do for You?

After Jesus fed the five thousand, he went to the mountain in retreat, and when he returned, he found the disciples looking for him. Christ told the disciples that they were looking for him not because of the signs he performed in feeding the five thousand but because of the food they ate. At which point he says, "Do not work for food that spoils, but for food that endures to eternal life" (John 6:27).

Good question for all Christian leaders. We need to avoid the self-serving leadership style. We get enticed, reinforced, encouraged by the secular world to think of ourselves, but Christ would encourage us to do the opposite. So how do you, as a Christian leader, inform the organizational management goals? That's where, perhaps, it gets harder as Christian leaders, because in a community-based organization like the one I lead, you can't put in corporate goals to lead people to Christ. That said, you have to find ways to integrate the secular with the sacred.

What happens for Christians is that our prayers, our focus, our heart may be different from the business world we sit in. So how do we bump up against that and influence that world without alienating others? Some Christians would say you are taking a wide-path leadership approach by not openly confronting people and being more aggressive with your faith. I hear that, and I get that, but that is not reality. You exemplify a Christ-inspired leadership approach through your actions. For me, how our organization addresses health equity and disparities and the societal factors influencing health and well-being are actions we have taken guided by my Christian faith, even though that has never been spoken in any way.

While never done intentionally, the executive leadership at the organization I lead now is a fairly strong faith-based group. And while you would not ask this question overtly, you wonder about whether you would hire someone who had a stronger faith or stronger business skills. We had a recent recruit for an executive position who was very open about her faith. She had tremendous expertise, but her honesty about her faith was impressive. It just adds another dimension to someone's portfolio. I was impressed, embarrassed, and envious at the same time. I wish I had been an example like her!

What is true for individuals is true for organizations.

Some Churches Are Just Not Helpful

Growing up in a very doctrine-focused world, there were lots of arguments about fine points of doctrine—like what's the right way to tithe, or what's the right way to think about the Lord's Last Supper, or how we should baptize. But these detailed discussions don't equip you well to go to work that day.

In the other extreme, there are churches that are all about positive thinking. Robert Schuller and Norman Vincent Peele are proponents of this positive approach. But for me, while I understand where they are coming from, that wasn't very helpful. God does not always have a wonderful plan for my life.

At one point in my career, a pastor told me that my work life was interfering with my church life and that I should quit and find another job that would allow me to spend more time in church. That wasn't very helpful since I had a family to support.

In the Great Commission (Matthew 28:16–20), Jesus Christ urges his disciples to "make disciples of all nations." What does that actually mean? How do you measure that? How strong should we be in attempting to fulfill that Great Commission? Does achieving this purpose have to be overt, and how do you maintain any sense of humility if you are overt? Does it mean adding more people in seats in church, as some megachurches seem to be concerned about, or is there a deeper meaning? And is that deeper meaning related more to leading by example to encourage people to have a genuine change of heart? The debate about the meaning of this verse creates significant tension in your life as you are navigating in a secular world.

I am guessing that I am not the only one who has wondered at times if some churches are really taking Christ's idea of ministering to people and bringing them along to faith and converting that approach to a strictly numbers game. In some of the megachurches Barbara and I have attended, there seems to be an overzealous focus on numbers. They measure Christmas services by how many attended, and through that metric, they plug in numbers about how many lives have been saved.

At one church we attended, I was helping to implement a Christian leadership series. I thought the response and discussion was great. There were anywhere from forty to seventy people who attended the series at any given session. People who were significant leaders in the community attended regularly, discussing Christ's leadership example. But the numbers weren't good enough for the church, so the series was canceled. One of the pastors commented it was a lot of work to set up tables and chairs for such small numbers. Many would rather have hundreds gather to hear secular leaders talk at a Christian-themed conference than minister to dozens in a local venue.

That is the society we live in. Corporate standards are being applied to faith and to the church and are held out as gold standards for the church to achieve. That is totally backward. When you read the Gospels, Christ never talked numbers with his people. Collecting and evaluating numbers is fine, but you have to have the change of heart first, because without that, the numbers are meaningless.

Can the Protestant Work Ethic Lead to Wide-Path Leadership?

Dwight L. Moody was an American Evangelist and publisher in the nineteenth century and was the founder of the Moody Bible Institute and Moody Publishers in Chicago, Illinois. One of his famous quotes is "Faith makes all things possible; love makes all things easy."[3] He gave up a lucrative boot and shoe business to devote his life to revivalism and established one of the major centers of evangelicalism in the nation in Chicago. He was a businessman in clerical clothes.

Some of the ideals of the Protestant work ethic were tied to a kind of natural corporate order, where if you operated by those principles, you could attain spiritual and material success. You work hard. You take care of your family. That is the Protestant work ethic, but then we don't connect it back to why we do this. It was kind of like corporate evangelicalism. Religious organizations began to look increasingly like corporations. In this sense, that work ethic, if we are not careful, can lead us down the path toward being a wide-path leader.

Similarly, the concept of the prosperity gospel, a belief among some Protestant Christians that financial blessing and physical well-being are always the will of God, sounds great but can quickly lead you down a very broad path. There is a challenge and a warning. You need to maintain that narrow path to be humble and thoughtful in your stewardship of resources, to make an impact with the resources and the faith you have.

This idea that if you are successful, God favors you is erroneous. The truth is that some of us, for whatever reason, have better opportunities than others. For example, I get a lot more credit than I deserve for things I do because I have a certain job, and because of that job, I have attained a certain amount of wealth. And because of this job, sometimes people are a lot more gracious to me than they need to be or should be. People should have been just as gracious to my dad, who had no money and no education.

The Hungry Sheep Look Up and Are Not Fed

John Milton was a seventeenth-century poet who wrote a poem titled "Lycidas" that took on the unfit shepherds of anti-Protestantism during his day. One line from the poem is often quoted: "The hungry sheep look up, and are not fed,/ But swol'n with wind, and the rank mist they draw,/Rot inwardly, and foul contagion spread."[4]

You are at the table, at church, and you are learning, and yet you are starving. You are starving for words you will hear on Sunday that apply to your life, especially from the leadership standpoint.

You go to church out of a sense of faith and obligation, but it is really not integrated into life and leadership. When you begin to integrate the two, you feel much more powerful.

Today, I pray to the Holy Spirit to guide my heart, my mind, and my thoughts. As part of that, I pray to bless the organization I currently lead because through this organization and its resources, we do great things in our communities. Does that mean we are going to succeed? No, because there are no guarantees. God's view of life, what's important, is different from our view. Our heartbreaking disappointments are not the same to God. That is hard stuff to consider. Our view of God, our view of Christ, should shape how we view life, but it is hard sometimes. Especially when it does not equal our views of success. Maybe we will fail. But you should have confidence. I am a sinner, I have weaknesses, but I am doing the best I can. I am not trying to enlist the Holy Spirit in what my plan is. But as I pray, I feel closer and more in touch with the Holy Spirit.

American Christian Institutions Are Becoming Corporations First

David French is an American political commentator who is also an evangelical Christian. In one of his recent posts, he laments that all too many American Christian institutions are corporations first.[5] I was talking to a pastor about recruiting new pastors, and one of the new, young pastors at the church did not have a theology background. He had a marketing background. The trend now, he said, is for churches is to hire MBAs who may not have faith background. It is all very corporatesque. To a point, this makes sense, but at some point, this corporate analysis becomes the measure of success. It's all about metrics, marketing, and performance. When you see this corporate view of religious success, chances are that is a wide-path approach.

You want to be relevant. You want to have opportunities to spread the Word. But not when it overcomes you. Christ didn't try to be relevant. Christ was relevant by his actions. He never flaunted his relevance. He lived the life he was called to live. And he came to shake things up.

It is the same thing when you look at the Pharisees and Sadducees. They did not do things in a Christian manner: the selling in the temples had nothing to do with faith; the rules they put in place had not a thing to do with the Christian faith. It had to do with controlling—or corporatizing in today's lingo—what Christianity was to be all about.

I am guessing that the tension I describe in these last several chapters has probably been felt by many of you, whether or not you identify as a Christian. We are all flawed human beings, and when you combine that with the imprecision of language, it can allow people to create a world where life is all about the "gospel according to me;" how science and scripture can be synced with success; how people who identify as Christian leaders may not actually be Christ-inspired leaders; and how individuals and organizations can quickly get on the wide path. We are all on a path whether we clearly see it or not. There are clearly times for all of us where we must redirect our lives to a Christ-inspired approach. The next chapter offers a few insights into how we might be able to move forward through some of that tension.

FIVE

MOVING FORWARD THROUGH THE TENSION

How do we move forward amid all these challenges and tensions we all face each day?

When I started to look at leadership and began to create my own summary and list of what leadership should be, I essentially used secular writings to inform and influence my leadership approach. It is easy to find yourself flat in the middle of that secular path because that's where most people are. It is what you hear at work, at conferences, from academics, from consultants, and at times even at church. But as we increasingly and intentionally follow a Christ-inspired leadership approach, we can consider what the secular offers while still distinguishing that we are following a different path for different reasons toward the same end goal. It is an approach that significantly impacted my day-to-day business decisions and my decisions in life.

In the introduction, I mentioned the example of two stacks of presentations I was working on—one for a secular audience, one for a Christian audience—and how the two presentations fell together. In truth, the two presentations should not have been separate. Christian and secular need to be together. There is a need to think about secular and business concepts through the lens of Christ's leadership example. It seemed the starting point should be from the Christ-inspired approach first, and then integrate that into the secular practice.

In his second book on how to move organizations from being good to being great, *Good to Great and the Social Sectors,* Jim Collins seems to come to a more Christian-center conclusion regarding how to achieve this goal.[1]

He suggests that it isn't how much money you make but how much impact you make relative to your resources. This is a wonderful statement because it really comes from a place of servant leadership (whether he intended to do this or not), and it shows how organizations and individuals should think about what resources they have and how to make an impact. Perhaps to make the statement more applicable to a truly Christ-inspired leadership approach, I might add one word: it's all about the impact you make relative to your *faith* and resources. You are given resources. You are given faith. Now what impact are you going to make with those resources and that faith? This is how you will be judged.

As Christian leaders, it is important to acknowledge and wrestle with the nuances of language and how words influence others.

We should test secular thought with the framework of our faith. We should source first from Christ and what he did, and then the secular.

We should not be apologists for science; nor should we see ourselves as rigid enforcers of scripture. Our points of reference should not only include scripture and historical context but also our reason, our experience, and, most importantly, the guidance of the Holy Spirit.

We should be confident in our Christianity and bring people along without needing to be overt.

We should not try to fit Jesus into a personalized mold of what we want him to be. There is no personalized spiritual whiteboard where we can write down what we want, and God will make that happen. The reverse is the truth. We should ask God how to fulfill his plan, not our personal list.

We should lead not by making moral judgments but rather by the grace of Jesus.

We should not focus only on the miracles of Christ but be led by the cross. We must move closer to Christ, not further from him, by becoming smaller and allowing Christ to be greater.

And a first step in accomplishing this, in finding ourselves and leading others, is to find a sense of transcendent purpose, which we discuss in the next chapter.

PART 2

Finding Myself, Leading Others

SIX

FINDING PURPOSE

Vic Strecher is a professor and director for innovation and social entrepreneurship at the University of Michigan School of Public Health, and he is the author of the book *Life on Purpose*.[1] We have become friends over the years and share many common interests. We first had the opportunity to meet as neighbors in a small community near Traverse City, Michigan. As we talked, Vic told me the story of his twenty-year-old daughter, Julia, who died suddenly as a result of a heart attack. The heart attack was at the end of a lifelong journey, because as a six-month-old in 1990, Julia had chicken pox that, among other things, attacked and destroyed her heart. She received a new heart on Valentine's Day, 1992, and Julia lived a full life up until the time of her sudden death.

Vic, his wife, and their family were understandably devastated by his daughter's death. He was rudderless and had lost meaning in his life. Then on one cold, early morning, Vic started out in his kayak on Lake Michigan, unclear where he was going or why. And as the sun broke over the horizon, Vic stopped paddling. And suddenly, he felt the warmth and the presence of his daughter. And she told him in no uncertain terms to "Get over yourself!" and try to find ways to help others.

From that transcendent moment, Vic's life took on renewed purpose. As a man of science, he couldn't explain what had just happened. But that story lays the foundation for his book, *Life on Purpose*. While a scientist writing about purpose or meaning in life, Vic often used terms that you might find in a Bible class. He talks about having a transcendent purpose in a way that is almost an act of worship—it is about something greater than yourself and finding your most "true" or "divine" self.

He notes the many benefits of having a strong sense of purpose, including doing better in life psychologically and socially compared to those without that strong belief. In addition, having a strong sense of purpose has been shown to slow the progression of Alzheimer's disease and is associated with an increase in natural killer cells that attack viruses and cancerous cells.

Unlike Vic, who had a singular moment that led to his transcendent purpose, I had a series of experiences over my life. I wore glasses as a young child, even before I went to school, and I had an optometrist, Bob Vermeer, who was very influential. My parents didn't have the luxury of going to school, and Bob was educated and wore a white coat, and he was somebody I spent a lot of time with as a young person. So I was this kid wearing glasses, which in those days wasn't an easy thing to do, but he was always incredibly encouraging and basically told me I could do whatever I wanted to do in life. One day in high school, we sat in his office, and he talked about purpose, potential, and having a "vision" for the future. I will never forget the day he told me that he believed that God had wonderful things planned for my life and that I should have "high" goals. My mother was an absolutely wonderful woman. I was five years younger than my brother and years younger than my sister. So in many ways, I was raised mostly as an only child. For most of my life, our kitchen had a thirty-cup percolator on the counter. I thought that was normal until I got in junior high. When friends came over, they would look at the percolator and ask if we were having a party. Coffee (and Dutch windmill cookies) was a social event, time to sit and talk. Breakfast, midmorning, lunch, midafternoon, and after dinner all involved coffee. It was a time to be together. I spent hundreds of hours drinking coffee with my mother, and I remember only uplifting, positive thoughts. She would say, "You are doing great!" "Your grades are awesome" (even if they weren't). "You can do great things." Let's just say I could do no wrong in my mother's eyes.

I had a very similar experience with my adviser in college, who often gave me some life lessons while advising about what classes to take. He encouraged me to think about getting a PhD in microbiology and teaching at a university, which I had never thought about. He was a nice, kindhearted man.

And then in one of my first jobs after graduate school, I had the privilege of occasionally traveling with Karl Wegner, MD, the founder of a successful clinical services company based in Sioux Falls, South Dakota. One day, flying in a small airplane to a public service hospital in South Dakota, he asked me a question that changed my life. He asked me what I was going to be doing in my fifties.

While the noise of the small plane made conversation a challenge, my response, "What?" was more about what are you asking me rather than indicating I couldn't hear him over the noise. His comment stunned a young twenty-eight-year-old just starting his career and a family. He said, "I will be disappointed if you are not aspiring to do something else." When the CEO of a growing company tells you to leave, it can be a bit confusing, especially to someone just starting their career.

Ultimately, I took the LSAT and was accepted into law school. Around the same time, I took a Christian counseling class and looked into health care, all as possible career choices.

And my wife would often remind me, "You always talk about being a lawyer, but do you think you would like to do what a lawyer does?" And I thought, *Oh yeah, good point. I don't think I want to do what they do.*

And after taking a Christian counseling class, I found that did not fit my personality.

So I ended up in health care administration. Basically, I went back to my Christian framework and thought about the path forward and what would fulfill my life purpose, and I never looked back.

So unlike Vic, I did not have a single event or interaction that created a transcending purpose (I am Dutch, so that is really not part of our demeanor), but what I did have was a series of events and people. Since those early years, I've had a series of bosses, some better than others, I've learned from along the way. But those three moments, those times as a young person, with the optometrist, my college adviser, and business associate, all helped lead me to my transcending purpose. You could argue that they were put in my life at that point to help me move me in the right direction.

While Vic focuses on things from a purely scientific/secular basis, and I focus on life from a Christian perspective, the outcome of what we are trying to achieve is often the same. But we do come at life differently. Vic comes at life perhaps from a personal perspective based on agents like theologians and researchers who create a philosophy of life. Always analyzing data. Trying to homogenize experience.

Christians differ in that they immediately have a leader in Christ to follow. And that, for me, in black and white, should be my absolute purpose.

We may both end up in the same place, but a key distinction is the afterlife. You believe that the only way you get that to happen is through faith. Then you look at purpose. And you see how important it can be in people's lives.

Vic tells the story about the two bricklayers. One bricklayer says that he is paid by the brick, and the other says he is building a cathedral. So perspective is critical in how you think about purpose. Do you want to be someone who is paid by the brick or someone who is building a cathedral? With all humility, I wanted to build a cathedral.

A couple of years ago, I was reading about how millennials are keenly interested in life purpose. They want to consider life purpose in how they navigate their lives. They want careers that are purposeful and to work in environments that have similar purposes. And the survey we conducted for this book clearly indicated that those who had a strong faith also felt they had a strong purpose in their lives. And that made me think of Vic, and I gave him a call about life purpose. That evolved into a discussion about purpose and the social determinants of health, which are socioeconomic factors that influence health and well-being, such as hunger, education, and financial stability. The organization I worked for screens all patients in primary care offices for ten different societal factors, but we had never screened for life purpose.

A health system can help address the clinical components of these social determinants of health. But if the person doesn't have a purpose or is not purposeful in his or her intent, that makes addressing these issues much more challenging. And as Vic and I talked about it, we thought there was something to continue to have a conversation about.

At that point, we brought the social determinants team into the discussion and basically said we are going to screen not only for social determinants but also life purpose. Initially, members of our team were a bit reluctant. But then Vic showed up to our offices and gave his presentation. And at that point, they were convinced it made sense.

Today, the organization is screening some of our employees, and also with a couple of companies, for life purpose, or personal determinants of health, as well as social determinants of health.

So fast-forward, and the organization has entered into a partnership with Vic's company, called Kumanu. Kumanu is rooted in several cultures and traditions. In Sanskrit, "manu" signals the birth of humanity. In Hawaiian, "kumu" invokes purpose. And in Maori, "kumanu" means to nurture and cherish. It is all about purpose in action. Kumanu offers an app-based product called Purposeful, which is a tool to reflect daily on how we are dealing with living out our life purpose.

Our social determinant product, Resourceful, supports employers by addressing previously unrecognized socioeconomic factors that can have a profound impact on an employees' quality of work and life. The rationale for this program is supported by a Harris Poll survey revealing that nearly a quarter of full-time workers in this country have experienced food insecurity and childcare issues, and one in five were worried about stable housing.[2] This program helps provide meaningful solutions to help employers and employees address these issues. Kind of a big idea.

This program will continue to evolve, but it illustrates the importance of life purpose and that however we come to life purpose, it is one key way we each navigate our lives.

Being able to articulate your life purpose can be hard, even for people who you would think would have a strong sense of purpose. One of my senior woman executives told me the story about her experience in facilitating a discussion group of fifty women leaders, many of whom were physicians. You might immediately think that this is a group of people who should have a strong sense of purpose. But when asked to articulate their life purpose, many of them just sat there, unable to say anything. It just floored all of us that these successful, extremely intelligent people were unable to articulate their life purpose. As the result of this conversation, the group spent some time focusing on what their life purpose might be.

What that tells you is that in many instances, people don't think in those terms, and often they have never been asked or had someone help them begin to think about and articulate their life purpose. In our hectic lives, we may not take time to reflect on life purpose, but when you follow Christ, you immediately have to define your life purpose.

For Christian leaders, you go back to your fundamental beliefs and look back at Christ's example. When I think about the Sermon on the Mount in Matthew and Sermon on the Plain in Luke, and the Beatitudes (all of which we discuss in more depth in subsequent chapters of the book) you have a clear understanding of who your focus should be on.

In times of crisis, as Christian leaders, we often have the best opportunity to achieve transcendental growth for ourselves and those around us. In the April 2002 issue of *Harvard Business Review*, Richard Boyatzis, Annie McKee, and Daniel Goleman wrote about "Reawakening Your Passion for Work."[3] The article appeared in the aftermath of the 9/11 attack. And they wrote about how, in times of crisis, people often take the opportunity to take a step back, think about their purpose in life, and seek to find something bigger than themselves. Something beyond what Peggy Lee sings about in the late 1960s pop song "Is That All There Is?"[4]

As the COVID-19 pandemic began to bear down on the country, and as a Christian leader, I saw it as a great opportunity to have a discussion about life purpose with our employees and board members across twenty-eight states. And that led to discussions with Vic, which resulted in a series of fireside chats where I interviewed Vic about life purpose. We ended up broadcasting three one-hour videos to all our 40,000 employees, 2,100 physicians, and our 500 community board members.

When we videotaped the fireside chats on life purpose, one of our videographers who shot the videos told me later that when he first started taping the interviews, he thought they would be incredibly boring, but he said afterward they were among the best videos we had ever done. Board members began sharing the videos with their kids and grandkids. Doctors emailed me to let me know it was just what they needed at the time to help reestablish purpose in their lives.

From a Christian leadership standpoint, it just seemed like a critical time to frame up the concept of life purpose. For me, having a framework and life purpose has been fundamental. Life will always change; there will always be a crisis at some point in your life. Having a clear life purpose has given me the confidence to remain fluid. No matter what I was doing or where I was going, I always had this solid core, this essential purpose. I always try to keep that fresh in my mind, because when I have, it has always been easier navigate the murky waters of life.

During our fireside chats and in his book, Vic talks about people needing to be in touch with their inner god or their true or divine self versus following a hedonistic approach to life.

And what you worry about from a faith standpoint and from the example of Christ's leadership, and as a Christian in general, is that you can get confused sometimes in a secular world. You go to educational conferences, and people talk about these other philosophies of life that can sound exciting. You have to be pretty disciplined from a faith perspective to keep on a Christ-inspired path. There are so many bumps in life that thinking about ways to ground yourself is critical. Prayer, reading scripture, meditation, small group discussions, or fellowship groups all have a grounding can all help. At the end of this book is an appendix, including Bible verses that can be used to help think about a Christ-inspired approach to leadership.

I think what happens for most Christians is they jump on the wide path because they think that's what they are supposed to do. They walk into big companies, and that's what they hear. So it is easy to see that is the way. And unfortunately, churches can reinforce some of these wide-path behaviors by working to apply business processes and practices to religion. But really, we shouldn't if we are disciplined believers. We have a clear example, a clear mission, a clear leader to follow. And often, as Christian leaders, we really haven't talked about it or laid it out there in a way that is helpful.

Max De Pree is one of my favorite writers, who we will talk more about later in this book. When the book *Leadership Is an Art* first came out, I used to give it to the managers who reported to me.[5] Max talks about the Protestant work ethic as a framework not only for leaders but for people in general. The concepts of temperance, resolution, frugality, industry, sincerity, and justice all provide a framework for living. And you could argue that for a majority of this country's existence, that Protestant work ethic has driven a lot of success that this country has had. But there has been erosion of some of these ideals in recent times. This is where it gets a little hard.

The way we grew up in Iowa was very much influenced by the Protestant work ethic. I started working at a very young age, in fifth grade. I bought my own clothes and other things like that and never felt bad about it. My parents gave us a tremendous life. But I made money. I got a job. I have worked my whole life. It was just something you did as a part of life. We grew up in a time where you kept your head down, kept your mouth shut, and worked hard. That clearly is influenced by the Protestant work ethic. And I still have that.

I feel very blessed in my life, with my family and in a role as a Christian leader where we can have an impact on the lives of so many people.

The next question I invariably ask myself is: *I am blessed, so what am I going to do about it? We have been given resources. What impact is God calling me to do with these resources?*

The work we are doing at our organization related to the social determinants of health and health inequities is beginning to get at the root causes of how to address health and well-being in this country, and the work is an extension of who I am as a Christian leader. It is definitely part of my life's purpose as a Christian.

There was a time I was being interviewed for a popular national health care podcast, and we were discussing my organization's focus on addressing socioeconomic factors that impact health, and the interviewer asked me, "Given your background, I assume this is motivated by religion, right?" And, while surprised he would say that, I replied, "Yeah, we just don't talk about it because we are not a religious-based organization."

But you don't have to overtly say that you are doing something as a result of faith; instead, you advocate by your actions. Addressing the social determinants is all about following Christ's leadership example and following the path set by the Sermon on the Mount.

In his book and in our fireside chats, Vic talks about the concepts of having a transcendent purpose, which is the concept of having an experience that is larger than life, an experience that has been described as being spiritual in nature, and then as a result of that experience, you alter your life purpose intentionally. Research has shown that oftentimes the more deeply we engage with religion, the greater our sense of purpose. Religion, faith, and purpose go hand in hand. For some people, living a good life and being a good person are enough. But as a person of faith and one who believes, that's not enough.

As the protests rose up around the country in response to the killing of George Floyd and other black people by police, giving rise to the Black Lives Matter movement, we heard from people wondering if the organization I lead was going to make a statement in support of the protests. We challenged our team by saying a statement is good, but more importantly, what are we going to do about it? That's the part that's a bit frustrating to me. People yak, but then nobody does anything. What are we going to do differently?

How can we do things differently? We will talk more about this in the chapter on finding perspective.

Each year, the public relations firm Edelman conducts national research on the subject of who and what Americans trust. And in recent survey results, in almost all areas, trust is at an all-time low. Trust in our institutions, trust in each other. There isn't much trust going around anywhere these days. Vic and I talked about the concept of trust and purpose during the fireside chats.

For Vic, trust is transcendent. He quotes researchers who suggests that we need to rise above our ego and transcend. And that sometimes to achieve that transcendental growth and purpose requires some kind of trauma or crisis. Vic is a university professor, and that is how his mind operates— always searching for answers. He is trying to seek the counsel of various philosophers and form them into a life mold, and that is a pretty challenging thing to do. For me, I am not sure how you do that.

It is actually much easier for Christians because our trust is all about trust in the Lord Jesus Christ and in the power of the Holy Spirit and in His words. We know what we trust, and we know what our purpose is. We trust in Christ's life, death, resurrection, and the resulting salvation for believers. And we can trust in Christ being *the* example of leadership.

Our purpose is activated by the example of Christ. And that should be enough. That should be the example, our purpose.

During our fireside chats, we talked about how some people are here to make money. And sometimes people get caught up in chasing the completion of tasks, and they don't think about what it is doing to them, ultimately wondering if this is all there is. Unfortunately, when people are all about chasing and achieving tasks instead of focusing on overall health and well-being, it can turn into a vicious cycle that can lead to a feeling of a lack of having a purpose. They are focused more on immediate gratification, and those things often don't relate to a bigger, broader sense of purpose.

For me personally, as a Christian leader, I've seen it happen more in the last couple of years. In health care, we chase all kinds of goals, many of them very important for clinical care. But when our purpose began to shift to addressing social determinants of health and health inequities, it began to force us to think about health and well-being in a very different manner. There is more than just taking care of people clinically. There is another deeper level.

So how do you derive your purpose? Like the doctors at our organization who couldn't immediately articulate their life purpose, and through the COVID pandemic, or like so many of us after 9/11, people wonder, *What am I doing with my life? Is this the way I want to live?*

People examine their priorities in life. It is too bad that it often requires trauma to push us to think about our life purpose.

How can we help people think about life purpose prior to a crisis? It should be a goal for every leader to have everyone who works for them to be able to articulate "this is what I am about, this is my purpose in life, this is why I am here." That would be pretty powerful.

At our organization, we have a tagline—"Your Health. Our Mission." And we recently discussed adding "My Purpose." We are thinking about how we can use that throughout the organization not just as a branding statement but as a way for people to think about their purpose throughout the organization. By doing that, it will help people to be happier and healthier.

Sometimes, as an organization, we tend to process things to death, so we are working through how we implement this as an organization. I wanted to have a sticker for everyone that would say "Ask me about my purpose." Some people thought it was a little aggressive. But it seemed to me potentially a great dialogue between a patient and a caregiver.

As a Christian, sometimes achieving your purpose requires both active and passive obedience. Christ's example is really interesting. Many people think about how active he was. But for parts of his life, he was very passive. He worked hard. He was a good son. He spent thirty years working as a carpenter, quietly studying scripture and preparing for his ministry. And then he became very active. And then, in just a few short years, he taught and led, he was brought to the cross, and he died.

In the quiet times, he took time to refresh, regenerate, and pray. He avoided trouble because it wasn't the right time. Even toward the end, there were times when he was very quiet and passive. People say that it was Pontius Pilate who crucified Jesus. But no, Jesus was set to die. Pontius Pilate just happened to be the way to do it. When Jesus was on trial, people said, he set all those things in motion, and his response was "That's what you say. So be it." They exhorted Jesus to defend himself. And he didn't, passively.

Even the crucifixion itself is a very passive act of obedience. And that led to one of the most transcendent moments in the history of humankind.

In 1986, the *Journal of the American Medical Association* (JAMA) published an article describing the physical death of Christ as he was crucified, based on a pathologist's analysis of biblical and historical text, supplemented by evidence from other archeological findings.[6] The article provides graphic detail about just how horrific the physical toll of the crucifixion must have been, from the deep lacerations and blood loss inflicted as a result of the public flogging, to Jesus sweating blood in the Garden of Gethsemane, to a vivid description of the path of the nails through the bones and nerves of Christ's wrists. Yet Christ knew his purpose, and he accepted God's will.

I think there's a lesson there for us all. There are times when we want to be very, very active in life. And there are other times you want to step back a little bit and be a little more passive in life. It's part of life; it's taking grace, it's physical, it's mental, it's spiritual. But Christ was a master of picking the right times to do things and act—and when not to.

In this chapter, we have talked about purpose and perhaps having a transcending purpose. It is good for your health. It is deeply valued. Your life purpose may be revealed by God in one transcendent moment, or it might be a series of events that you don't even realize are connected. And it is a dynamic process.

From a faith standpoint, we would say that our life purpose comes from God. It's clear, and it is what it is. Our understanding of our purpose and putting it into our life in the context of how and where we want to accomplish it is critical. We search our souls and look for life purpose in a variety of ways. As Christians, it is from the example of Christ. That's the purpose we are called to.

We can certainly agree with our secular friends about some of the process, yet we have a definitive answer. I would never have expected that many of my discussions about life purpose with Vic, my colleagues, my mentors, and others would involve discussions about my faith and how it impacts my purpose.

Here are some things we know. Purpose is not about prestige or legacy, because finding a life purpose can be found in the simple, the mundane.

Purpose can bring tremendous joy. And as a Christian leader, you believe that purpose is not up to you, that it comes from Christ and God. When you think about how Christ articulated his life purpose, you look at how those concepts and ideals align with what Christ is asking us to do. It is one thing to have purpose, but does the life purpose align with what Christ has in mind for us? In the research done about the impact of life purpose, it is clear that purpose drives engagement, resiliency, and retention. One of the keys is to help an individual align their personal purpose with that of the organization. For me, that alignment comes in addressing the social determinants in people's lives.

When thinking about purpose, think about the bricklayer we discussed earlier in this chapter. Do you want to be the bricklayer who wants to be paid by the brick or the bricklayer who is building a cathedral?

We are blessed. How do we use that blessing? What are we going to do about it? Our purpose should always align with Christ's mission and values. Can an organization have a transcending purpose as it lives its mission and vision? That is something for consideration in the next chapter.

SEVEN

LIVING MISSION

Finding a purpose and then having and living a mission are closely connected. They both relate directly to our reason for being. In today's world, you might actually wonder what the difference is. A distinction might be that when people think about purpose, they might think about an individual first, and when you think about mission, people might tend to think first about businesses. In a biblical sense, mission means to send, which makes complete sense when you think about the Great Commission: "Therefore, go and make disciples of all the nations" (Matthew 28:19). In truth, missions and values can relate to both individuals and organizations. Organizations perhaps are more overt about sharing their mission with the publics they serve.

One thing is clear. Some of the best ways to help reduce the anxiety created by the tensions felt between the sacred and secular worlds, or just by the world in general, is to have a clear purpose, an identified mission, and strong values you use every day to complete the purpose and mission.

Even though he didn't describe it as such, Christ had a clear mission and concrete values by which he achieved that mission.

Just to be sure we are all off on the right footing for this chapter, it might be helpful to briefly define what I am talking about when I use the words *mission* and *values*.

Think about mission as a person's or an organization's reason for being. A *mission statement* is usually a short statement that defines why an organization exists, what its goal is, and what it desires to be. The mission statement is the way the organization communicates purpose and intent to the world. Mission statements are fairly stable and often exist unchanged for many years. For example, Tesla's mission statement is "to accelerate the world's transition to sustainable energy." The mission of the organization I work for is to "improve your health and well-being."

The *values of the organization* are often thought of as the ideals that describe the heart of the organization. The values reflect that mission and the vision statement and let employees and other audiences understand what the organization stands for and the behaviors they intend to display. *Values drive behavior* and provides a check to the way decisions are considered and made. The goal is for employees to understand the values and embrace them as the way business is done. It illustrates acceptable and desired behavior and, on the flip side, what is unacceptable. Think about values as the *how* organizations will achieve their missions. Values help to provide a moral compass as to how the company and its employees will conduct themselves. Missions are focused on direction, while values are about integrity.

Values statements are clearly identified. Often you will see statements that list desired values like stewardship, integrity, and respect.

Tesla's core values are doing the best, taking risks, constant learning, and environmental consciousness. My company's core values are compassion, innovation, teamwork, and excellence.

A Suggested Mission and Values of Christ

When you think about how Christians might define Christ's mission and values, you start with God's mission for Christ, which was to save us from our sins. This is a mission that would be completed not only through Christ's life and death but also through the guidance of the Holy Spirit.

Understanding that there can be, and has been, debate by many learned scholars, what follows is a best attempt at Christ's mission and values and how we might apply them in our daily lives and as Christian leaders.

God's Mission for Christ
- To save us from our sins (John 3:17).

Christ's Mission for Us
- "To go and make disciples of all nations, baptizing them in the name of the Father, and of the Son, and of the Holy Spirit, and teaching them to obey everything I have commanded you" (Matthew 28:16–20) (The Great Commission).

Christ's Values
- Love the Lord your God with your heart, soul, and mind (Matthew 22:35–39) (The Great Commandment).
- Love your neighbor as yourself (Matthew 22:35–39 (The Great Commandment).
- Live the Beatitudes (Matthew 5:3–12).

The Antivalues
- The woes of the Pharisees (Matthew 23, verses 13–16, 23, 25, 27, and 29).

How Do We Bring Christ's Mission for Us to Life?

We will be talking in greater depth about the how we can achieve Christ's mission to make fishers of men in the chapters on leading change and leadership development.

As we discussed in an earlier chapter, I was really impressed and influenced by the Jim Collins's *Good to Great and the Social Sectors: Why Business Thinking Is Not the Answer,* where he wrote that our success will be determined by the impact we make relative to our resources.[1] I believe I will be judged by my resources and the opportunities I have been given and what I did with them.

Christ's mission was to save us from our sins. You can argue that his mission for us is identified in the Great Commission, where he says, "Go and Make Disciples." He wants everyone to come to faith. God wants everyone to come to know Christ as our savior, in order to have their sins forgiven and go to heaven.

What he commands us to do is to live a Christian life, focusing on the Beatitudes, really with an idea of shaping your life so you can spread the good news.

The uncomfortable part as a Christian is how do you actually do that? Do you do it aggressively? Do you get in people's faces, or do you try to minister to them by example? Right or wrong, I have always looked for more subtle opportunities. I have never felt the overt, in-your-face sort of approach to be very effective. By and large, you can begin to steer people toward faith if you do it carefully and with humility and respect. Perhaps because of my Dutch reformed background, I have been more reserved and have never worn my religion on my sleeve, but as I have gotten older and in greater positions of authority, when I have had opportunities to talk about my faith, I feel more comfortable doing that.

To some extent, I like to think, *Wear the hat you are given in life.* Some will be quick to criticize people for not thinking more broadly about the growth of the company instead of focusing on their own little area of responsibility. Some may feel they don't have permission to do broader things. So, as a Christian leader, you have to give them permission. When I began taking on senior leadership positions, I would always think, *Tie your top button. Stroll to the podium.* And get going with the work at hand. Given the hat you wear, you also need to articulate a vision, create an urgency to change, and thank people along the way. When you have that hat and the opportunity to wear it, you need to embrace it! Everyone has different hats, and we all have different resources. But we can all minister utilizing the resources we have in our own ways.

Preparation and how you frame up your Christian leadership approach is critical to how you begin to achieve Christ's mission. Of course, you study, you listen, you learn, you pray. That is almost like a Christian checklist. Then you can extend these practices. I pray now more on my knees than I ever have before, and that is a very grounding experience. I have a spouse who is incredibly supportive. But it is more than that. It is how we proclaim Jesus in our actions and our words.

Defining "Neighbor"

The Great Commandment, which includes the first two values we should consider as Christian leaders, is made of two parts. The first value is to love the Lord with all your heart, soul, and mind, and the second value is to love your neighbor as yourself.

The first commandment, or value, is applied by living the mission, and we will spend the rest of this book defining how you do that. We will also spend time talking about the second value throughout the book. But the synoptic Gospels (the Gospels according to Mark, Matthew, and Luke) all say slightly different things about this commandment, and I wanted to spend a brief moment discussing that topic.

John's poetic "My command is this: Love each other as I have loved you" (John 15:12) is interesting because he does not use the word *neighbor,* as do Mark and Matthew: "Love your neighbor as yourself" (Mark 12:31, Matthew 22:39). Luke combines the two values in the Great Commandment, saying, "You shall love the Lord your God with all your heart, and with all your soul, and with all your strength, and with all your mind; and your neighbor as yourself."

So how are we supposed to consider the second half of the Great Commandment? How do you define *neighbor*? When you look at the historic context, a neighbor might have been defined literally as the person next to you or the country next to you. But as Christ refined scripture, he added a broader context to suggest that a neighbor can mean literally anyone.

At one point, Jesus is asked to define what being a neighbor means (Luke 10:29). Christ responds with the parable of the good Samaritan. A man is traveling from Jerusalem to Jericho, when he is attacked by robbers. Several people pass by and do not help. Then a Samaritan comes across the man, bandages his wounds, puts the robbed man on his own donkey, brings him to an inn and cares for him, and later pays the innkeeper to continue to care for him after the Samaritan has to leave. In truth, we are all neighbors. And we all have a responsibility to take action to care for others.

Living the Beatitudes

Christ outlines eight Beatitudes, or blessings, in the Gospel according to Matthew.

> Blessed are the poor in spirit,
> for theirs is the Kingdom of Heaven.

Blessed are those who mourn,
for they will be comforted.
Blessed are the meek,
for they will inherit the Earth.
Blessed are those who hunger and thirst for righteousness,
for they will be filled.
Blessed are the merciful,
for they will be shown mercy.
Blessed are the pure in heart,
for they will see God.
Blessed are the peacemakers,
for they will be called children of God.
Blessed are those who are persecuted because of righteousness,
for theirs is the Kingdom of Heaven.

Implicit in the concept of living the Beatitudes is to adopt a servant leadership approach where, as a Christian leader, the last becomes first, and the first becomes last (Matthew 19:30).

When you read the Beatitudes, if you paused every morning to look at them anew and then went forward every day to live by the example of the Beatitudes, that's pretty powerful. Translating these blessings to a Christian leadership value approach means being humble, merciful, pure in heart, and helping others, to mention just a few key characteristics.

To some, the Beatitudes may seem like soft actions or values. In truth, these are hardcore actions that can be challenging to accomplish in today's environment. Christ did these things in very demonstrative ways, and yet he exhibited the qualities of humility in how he treated people. He was a driven leader. He had a clear purpose and mission. A clear timeline. He was on a mission. It is important to remember that he embraced children, the disabled, women, and the poverty stricken. He was humble, he washed people's feet, and he took on figures of authority. He was compassionate in helping a poor widow and raising her only son from the dead; he healed lepers so they could get back to work; he healed people who were suffering physically; he freed the oppressed. These are not soft things; they are character pillars. He was able to do his job so well because he had these personal values.

The cost of living these values can be extreme. "Do you think I came to bring peace on earth? No, I tell you, but division" (Luke 12:51). Christ was calling out the leaders of the day—and their man-made rather than God-given rule—and forcing people to make choices. That is all part of the narrow path. Some will believe; some won't. He was doing good things in a new and challenging way. They are more than nice things to do. This is a leader, a militant, who looked out for those who couldn't look out for themselves. This is the leadership example we should hold up and that we should talk about and follow.

The Beatitudes help define a narrow path as Christian leaders. There are people who are only focused on how much money they can make. They would look at people who live the Beatitudes and say, "What a bunch of losers." They want to crush you. To dominate you. These are not Christian values. Christ was anything like a loser; he was a strong leader with a powerful personality. Yet he looked out for those who couldn't look out for themselves. You can be strong at heart and be compassionate toward people. You are looking to bring people with you, to lift people up. And that is the hard sort of leadership example and mission challenge that Christ set.

The Poor or the Poor in Spirit

While the listing of the Beatitudes in Matthew and Luke are mostly similar, some differences provide some interesting fodder for Christian leaders to consider.

For example, in Matthew, the verse reads, "Blessed are the poor in spirit," whereas in Luke, the verse says, "Blessed are you who are poor." The first focuses on the spirit, while the second seems to focus more on those who suffer poverty and financial hardships. As Christian leaders, we should consider both the financial and spiritual aspects. We will discuss this in greater detail in the chapters to come, but as a leader of a non-faith-based organization, my focus has increasingly been on helping those who have suffered health disparities and inequities, particularly in different aspects related to financial security, housing security, and poverty.

Being poor in spirit is all about being humble. The danger of leadership is that you can begin to feel like you are entitled to things or that you deserve something. Being poor in spirit is the idea that you are doing the best you can. You try to keep yourself lowly in your own eyes. You do work without acknowledgment. It is all about what your motivation is and taking a servant leadership approach. When I hear from hospital leaders about what they deserve, that is not the servant leader approach or being poor in spirit. You have to keep yourself honest. It is by the grace of God that you have a position of leadership. Be humble in that position. Be spiritually bankrupt before God.

If a blessing or talent is underappreciated or underused, then the blessing is wasted. Everyone is a debtor. You have no ability to make up for the gifts God gave you. You are saved. You are poor physically, mentally, financially, and spiritually without God. Any idea that you are above someone else is wrong.

The Antivalues

The Gospels not only suggest the kind of values we should strive for through the Beatitudes and the Great Commandment; they have kind of antivalues or behaviors/actions we should be careful about.

There are eight woes of the Pharisees found in Matthew 23, verses 13–16, 23, 25, 27, and 29. There are six in Luke. The woes largely criticize the Pharisees for their hypocrisy and perjury and illustrate moral and ethical concepts. The Pharisees taught about God but did not love Him. They taught law but did not practice justice, mercy, or faithfulness to God. Outwardly, they appeared clean, but they were tarnished internally. They pretended to be righteous but were the opposite.

Six Contemporary Beatitudes

Pope Francis, on All Saints Day in 2016, proposed six modern Beatitudes[2]:

1. Blessed are those who remain faithful while enduring evils inflicted on them by others and forgive them.
2. Blessed are those who look into the eyes of the abandoned and marginalized and show them their closeness.
3. Blessed are those who see God in every person and strive to make other also discover him.

4. Blessed are those who protect and care for our common home.

5. Blessed are those who renounce their own comfort in order to help others.

6. Blessed are those who pray and work for full communion between Christians.[2]

When you compare these Beatitudes against the Beatitudes in the Gospel according to Matthew, the sentiment and meaning in these contemporary Beatitudes in many ways corresponds to Matthew. Articulating the Beatitudes in this fashion has value. If you read those every day, they hopefully help you set your daily attitude.

Whether you are Protestant or a Catholic, another religion, or a person who is not sure what they believe, considering these Beatitudes provides you a structure and a point of view. You look at faith in all kinds of ways and how we are going to apply it.

Defining Reality through Mission and Values

Mission, vision, and values connect to purpose. When you begin to look at your personal purpose and Christ's mission, vision he had, the way he lived, and the values he exemplified, you can then combine your purpose with Christ's purpose and find ways to emulate that type of behavior.

As leaders, we need to think about what the reality of our lives is and what we are about. What is the reality of what is going to feed our soul? As Christian who are leaders, that reality would be through Christ.

As you define reality, the challenge is to not be influenced by a wide-path approach. It is hard when you see political, corporate, or community leaders who have tremendous opportunities, and they say the right religious things, but the reality is that many do not use their leadership opportunity. It is hard to stay on that narrow path and be authentic and true. People make mistakes. They begin to think they deserve things. And Christ never did. He lived on the narrow path. And from time to time, the path gets narrower, sometimes broader. We all jump on the broad path from time to time, but we have to bring ourselves back down.

The mission and values of corporate American continue to evolve. For example, KPMG is an international consulting company that helps organizations improve business performance, and in one particular research project, they compared the results of surveys with global CEOs about company priorities before COVID-19 and then during the pandemic.[3] The research showed that the agenda of CEOs radically shifted since the beginning of the pandemic. Bill Thomas, global chairman and CEO of KPMG, suggested that the crisis accelerated strategies that were already in place regarding social responsibilities, that people are more attracted to their organization's purpose and reasons for being and using this to guide their decisions.

Historically, the stated purpose of business was largely taken from the Milton Friedman view of business. The goal was clear: to make money for stakeholders.[4] In 2019, that principle of corporate governance was changed by the Business Roundtable.[5] It now reads: "Americans deserve an economy that allows each person to succeed through hard work and creativity and to lead a life of meaning and dignity."

When you evaluate these statements and these actions, you could argue that the concept of social responsibility and the revision to the Business Roundtable statement about the purpose of a corporation are influenced by the core of the Sermon on the Mount and the Beatitudes. People can lead a life of meaning and dignity when they are socially responsible, have compassion, are humble, and address the needs of others—whether it is diversity, inclusion, structural racism, people living in poverty, the disabled, or others in need. Maybe this change wasn't influenced by scripture, but it sure adopted a Christian perspective.

A Personal Journey to Living Mission

Early in my professional career, I remember starting my master's program at the University of Minnesota, and I was really taken aback by some of the ambitions of some of my younger classmates. Many had set dates in their minds about when they were going to be CEOs of major national corporations; they were going to run the world. And I am thinking, *Boy, that is kind of cocky.*

My road was a little slower. At first, my career mission was to get on a career path, take care of my family, and stop traveling. As I began to get opportunities in management, I was drawn to strategic planning, and over the years, I became the development and strategy guy wherever I went. It was something I was good at. I didn't really think about it as strategic planning. I really thought about it more as common sense. Always thinking about what's next? How do we focus people next?

My career has afforded me the opportunity to work in strategic planning for many years. As a strategic planner, you have no authority, but at the same time, you have all the authority in the organization. Your success, and to some extent the organization's, depends on your ability to influence thinking and decision-making. When you think about strategy, you really have an opportunity to put your fingerprint on something.

Strategic planning is part art and part science. During my career, it was one of the most enjoyable parts of my various jobs. Kicking off any strategic planning process starts at a high level with articulating the mission, vision, and values of the organization.

The words roll right off of any leader's lips—mission, vision, values— often expressed in buzzwords and corporate speak that we learn throughout our careers. They are our go-to thoughts in interviews and part of the bible of corporate America. These values populate our websites, our boardrooms, and our annual reports. The concern is: are these words real or just window dressing and leadership speak? No organization or leader of a business would ever admit they aren't real, of course.

In my last 13 years as president and CEO, I felt like I had more of an opportunity to include my value set into what we did as an organization. I felt like I have had more freedom to think about things in how they related to my faith and how to use my faith to shape the narrative of the organization. Our work related to addressing food insecurity and access to food or our work as anchor institution related to economic development in communities and neighborhoods where there is great need are just a couple of examples.

Christ's Mission Helped Him Focus from a Very Early Age

While finding my purpose and mission developed over time, Christ had a single-minded sense of direction, even at a very early age. Luke 2:41–49 relays the story of how Jesus, just twelve years old, had traveled with his parents and a caravan of people to Jerusalem for the Passover feast. After the feast, Joseph and Mary, along with friends and relatives, headed home. Jesus stayed. It wasn't until a day later that Joseph and Mary realized Jesus was not with them. They returned and three days later found Christ in the Temple courtyard, conversing with teachers. Mary, understandably upset, asked Jesus why he had stayed behind. His response: "Didn't you know I had to be in my Father's House?" (Luke 2:49). So even at this young age, Jesus had a clear purpose and direction. He may not have consciously comprehended that he was on a mission at that age. Yet he would not be distracted.

I am sure Mary and Joseph wondered at that point, "What kind of kid do we have on our hands here?" Even at this young age, Jesus was suggesting, "Why would you worry? I am in my Father's house, really doing my purpose." Christ was clearly on a path, and he kept learning and listening.

Thinking about Christ's Values as You Think about Which Company to Join and When to Leave

If you are looking for a job and you find a position you might be interested in with a particular organization, one of the first things you want to do is to check out the company's values and then compare them to your personal values. If they don't match up, you might want to look somewhere else for that new job. If you are Christian, you need to consider not only how a company intends to live its mission but also how it intends to do that and compare them against Christian values.

Here is a chart where you can look at my suggested mission and values of Christ. Then there is a column for you to list your values, and then there are core values listed by a few major corporations in this country. If you repeat this exercise with other organizations you might be considering working for, you can eliminate some prospects pretty quickly.

Compare/Contrast Christ's Values to Your Values and Organizational Values

Christ's Values	Your Values	American Express	Kellogg's	P&G	Zappos
• "Love the Lord your God with your heart, soul, and mind" (Matthew 22:35–39). • "Love your neighbor as yourself" (Matthew 22:35–39). • "Live the Beatitudes" (Matthew 5:3–12).		• We deliver for our customers. • We make it great. • We do what's right. • We respect people. • We need different views. • We win as a team. • We care about our communities.	• We act with integrity and show respect. • We are all accountable. • We are passionate about our business, our brands, and our food. • We have the humility and hunger to learn. • We strive for simplicity. • We love success.	• Integrity • Leadership • Ownership • Passion for winning • Trust	• Deliver WOW through service. • Embrace and drive change. • Create fun and a little weirdness. • Be adventurous, creative, and open-minded. • Pursue growth and learning. • Build open and honest relationships with communication. • Build a positive team and family spirit. • Do more with less. • Be passionate and determined. • Be humble.

Once you are in a company, sometimes you have to play the hand you are dealt. The company may have admirable values, but what happens when the CEO says the right things but doesn't live by the values? You either have to figure out a way to navigate the situation, or you have to get out. That is often not an easy decision, because you are considering many things beyond yourself, most significantly your family if you have one.

During my career, I once worked for an outstanding but challenging CEO, and I found myself with opportunities to leave the organization. I was at a crossroads. My CEO and I actually agreed a lot on strategy, but we disagreed on how to do things and what motivated our actions as a company. Facing an opportunity to leave, we had a very open and direct conversation where I pointed out my concerns, and we made a series of commitments to each other. We honored our commitments, I stayed, and we never spoke about it again.

That was a purifying experience for me. My faith was important as a foundation as I considered my options. It wasn't just about our end goals. It was about my values—my Christian values—in how we accomplished our mission. It was about our behavior as an organization and how we acted.

Sticking to your values gets easier as you progress in your career. When you are young, early in your career, you don't have confidence yet, so you just keep your head down and do your job, and then as you mature as a person and as a Christian, the opportunities to figure out to use your faith grow as well.

The poet T. S. Eliot wrote in "Four Quartets," "For us, there is only the trying, the rest is not our business."[6] As a Christian leader, that rings so true. You begin to realize that we are always limited, incomplete leaders and that only through the grace of God we continue to move forward in our mission.

Considerations and Questions

Early in this chapter, I provided a suggested mission and values of Christ. I have used these suggested values each day in helping achieve my life's mission:

- Love the Lord your God with your heart, soul, and mind (Matthew 22:35–39) (the Great Commandment).

- Love your neighbor as yourself (Matthew 22:35–39) (the Great Commandment).
- Live the Beatitudes (Matthew 5:3–12).

Every day, I think about how I live these values.

As discussed earlier in this chapter, some might consider the Beatitudes as soft values. In fact, they help define a very certain, very narrow path that requires great discipline to achieve. We live in a society where some think the only way to win is through intimidation and crushing competitors. These are people who live a life similar to the Pharisees, who were hypocrites; they taught about God and the law but did not practice justice, mercy, or faithfulness to God. They appeared righteous but were the opposite. Instead, be strong at heart and be compassionate toward people. Consider how to bring people along and lift up people.

EIGHT

SERVANT LEADERSHIP:
THE LAST IS FIRST; THE FIRST IS LAST

There were a number of secular leadership experts who helped frame how I think about leadership and Christian leadership. And whether intended or not, they all had a clear connection to and were influenced by the leadership of Christ.

Robert Greenleaf was a corporate director for management development, most notably at AT&T, one of the largest corporations in the country at the time, from 1929 through the 1960s. At AT&T, he implemented some truly progressive management-training programs, preaching at the time that organizations existed for the person as much as the person exists for the organization. He helped change how organizations thought about leadership. But it wasn't until after he retired from a career that Greenleaf became widely recognized as an expert in management development. In 1970, he published an essay titled "The Servant Leader."[1]

The main tenet of his concept of servant leadership is that it begins first and foremost with the feeling that we want to serve.

Greenleaf always acknowledged his work was informed by a Judeo-Christian work ethic. In fact, he became a Quaker in midlife. But his connection to the leadership example and teaching of Jesus Christ is immediate and striking. While Greenleaf is credited with coining the phrase, *everything you read in the Gospels is that Jesus Christ not only talked about servant leadership, he lived it.* Greenleaf took the concept of servant leadership and secularized it, but the thought came through Christ.

In Mark 9:35, Jesus called the disciples together and said, "Anyone who wants to be first must be the very last, and the servant of all." Similarly, in Matthew 20, Christ tells them, "So the last shall be first, and the first last: for many be called, but few chosen." Luke (22:26) interprets this same moment with James and John this way: "But you are not to be like that. Instead, the greatest among you should be like the youngest, and the one who rules like the one who serves."

The motivation to lead changes completely when you begin to think about the leadership example of Christ as servant leader. The motivation is not to be in charge. The motivation is to serve. Throughout my career, I have seen people who say they want to be in charge. At some point, we may all go through that thinking. *I want to make the decisions.* Sometimes it is about power, and sometimes it is about money. And sometimes it's a belief that they are naturally born leaders. But that is the principal motivation for many people, sadly.

There are some key characteristics of servant leaders that can easily be found in the Gospels of Mark, Luke, and John, and particularly in Matthew through the Sermon on the Mount and the Beatitudes.

Through the Beatitudes, Jesus teaches his disciples that blessed are those who mourn, are meek, hunger and thirst for righteousness, are merciful, are pure in heart, are the peacemakers, and are persecuted because of righteousness.

I think servant leadership starts with humility and meekness and includes being merciful and having compassion for others. Some might interpret that as being weak, but being humble and meek doesn't correlate with weakness, because that was who Christ was.

Most of us have worked with or for egocentric, ego-driven leaders. When I was in graduate school, several of my fellow students were very bright, but their clear intention was to be the boss, the person in charge, the person at the top making the decisions. And that was how they were going to measure their success in life.

When we do 360 leadership evaluations, we can quickly see those who are ego driven. They think they are already prepared to be CEO, thinking, *I could do that job today. I don't need more experience, mentoring, or training.* That outsized ego takes them on a wide path that can lead to disaster.

A favorite *Harvard Business Review* article of mine is "The Incomplete Leader," by Deborah Ancona, Thomas Malone, Wanda Orlikowski, and Peter Senge.[2] The main point of the article is that we are all incomplete leaders, and you are never truly complete. In that way, you are always a servant, and there are always things you can work on to be a better leader. It is the meekness, the humility, and the compassion shown by Christ that allows people to really strive to be better and keep on.

Philippians 2:3–4 says, "Do nothing out of selfish ambition or vain conceit. Rather, in humility value others above yourselves, not looking to your own interests but each of you to the interests of the others. Never think that something you have gotten in life is something that you deserve or is owed to you."

That verse is consistent with being the incomplete leader. We are missing parts, and that is really our life. We all have egos and get caught up in ourselves, so we need to take a step back. You fill in those parts by caring about others. We are and always will be incomplete leaders.

Those are always the fears at work. As you have more success and gain influence in your career, you need to be increasingly aware of how success impacts you. It is easy to begin to think you deserve something as you get used to this new way of life. And the higher up you go, the easier it is to think that way. You combat that by trying to stay grounded. It helps to have a family and significant other who stays grounded and keeps you grounded. You want to always remember where you came from, and if you focus on the notion that you are incomplete, it can help keep you balanced. We all make mistakes in our lives, sometimes big mistakes, and hopefully we are able to learn from them and move on.

For me, it is always going back to the principles of faith and what we are called upon to do. And when you are given an opportunity, you are accountable for the opportunity and the resources you have at your disposal. Someday we are all going to have to answer for the opportunity we had and what we did with that opportunity. Did we use the resources and talents we were given and think about how to apply the lessons learned from the Beatitudes and the Sermon on the Mount in our daily lives?

Max De Pree was the former CEO of Herman Miller, and after he retired, he became the best-selling author of a number of books on leadership: *Leadership Is an Art, Leadership Jazz,* and *Leadership without Power.*[3] Herman

Miller is based in western Michigan, and it is a large base for the Dutch community.

He has said that leadership is about three concepts: The first responsibility of a leader is to define reality. The last is to say thank you. In between, the leader is a servant.

There is an interesting passage in *Leadership Is an Art* where De Pree talks about discovering that a millwright at one of the company factories—a critical person in the factory who works with the machinery and manufacturing processes—was also a poet.[3] De Pree wonders if this person is a poet who works at a factory or a factory worker who happens to write poetry. He was trying to understand the essence of this person. And that is what good leaders do; they try to listen, understand the person's reality, and respect and appreciate the person for what they do—whether that is in work or in the community. This is what Christ did throughout his ministry as he interacted with people. He met people where they were at. He knew their life story and the challenges they faced, which is a great example for all leaders. It is important to take the time to know the life story of those who work with you. It will allow you to lead much more effectively.

De Pree talks about corporate leadership and how leaders owe a covenant to the company. The notion is almost a servanthood to the company itself. You have a special bond that exists between you and the company, and it is not what the company can do for you; it is what you can do for the company. When you start looking at this agreement, you are bound in some ways in your service back to the company. It is a solemn, binding agreement that you have. It is an interesting word to choose. It is a pledge. It is a contract.

Increasingly, I have thought about work as something sacred and that it is connected to the teachings and example of Christ. Viewing work and leadership as sacred helps you set it apart from the secular and establish a view of work that is dedicated to the examples of Christ. As some people retire and you talk to them, some of them talk about what the organization owed them; that is an example of a noncovenant relationship. With the idea of a covenant, you have a binding pledge with the company for what it has done for you.

I didn't own the organization I worked for. I could bring certain things to the organization. I was mindful of this. When we had to make an organizational decision to accept the transfer of patients who had medical complications after abortions at a local clinic, that wasn't my decision to make; it was ultimately the parent board's decision. I got some nastiness from religious people, but that's all right. People have different views on this issue, and we serve everyone, so it doesn't matter what my personal belief is; it is not my job to tell people what is right and what is wrong.

One Bible verse that helps me through situations like this is Matthew 7:1–2: "Do not judge, or you too will be judged." Sometimes people make strong, harsh judgments about people and their lives, and yet we try to decide which sins are more important than others. The Bible doesn't prioritize sins. We do that. Sometimes we take certain sins and say these are nonstarters. I certainly agree with the adage, the older you get, you realize the less you know. I look at Christ's example; what he said was "sin no more." Just stop what you are doing and try to lead a better life. What sometimes turns off people to Christians is the perception that they believe they are so much better than others. We try to be better, and we shouldn't judge others. Whatever some in society consider to be sins, I am not sure Christ deals with that any differently than when I have my daily list of sins. So how can you judge others? I was brought up believing certain actions were sinful, but as you mature as a Christian, you realize that so much of what we do is sinful. So how do you judge certain sins and ignore others? The older I get, the less (hopefully) I judge others.

Over the time of recorded history, Christians have opposed preventing and terminating pregnancies; at the same time, there is a history of providing these services. Is there a right answer? That depends on who you ask. It is easy to rationalize and judge people. And in our judgment, we lose all aspects of Christ's love. The question is, how do we treat each other civilly while having disagreements? We need to get back on the path. Be gracious.

Can an Institution Act as a Servant Leader?

As an extension of the organizational leadership of an organization, institutions can be servant leaders with a community work focus. It is an opportunity to use the institution in a significant, perhaps nontraditional way, to really do good things and make a very significant impact on the community and lives. The question is, to what degree are you willing to do that in your organization? Is it minimal? Superficial? What resources are you prepared to use to achieve a maximum change? Or is it something significant? So yes, organizations can be servant leader–based organizations.

In Jim Collins's book, *Good to Great and the Social Sectors*, the proposition he makes is that it is not how much money you make as an organization; it is the impact you make relative to your resources over a long period of time. So that's the question for every company. If organizations can start to make an impact with the resources available, you can really start to change people's lives. And Max De Pree says something similar in *Leadership Is an Art*, that "corporations should have a redemptive purpose," which is so true in that it is saying we have to have a greater purpose than its survival.[4] As individuals, we are all given opportunities to do different things, so what have we done with those opportunities? If you are in a position of influence, or do the things we are doing in a free country, what are you doing for the greater good and not just for yourself? If you call it servant leadership, or treating people with respect, the Beatitudes and how you treat others is what life is about. This is the example of Christ's leadership.

As I mentioned earlier, at the organization where I was CEO, we were on a journey in addressing the social determinants of health or the societal factors that influence health and well-being beyond clinical factors. These factors include poverty and financial security, hunger security, education, stable housing, and environmental issues.

As an organization, we began our approach to addressing the social determinants of health with an initial focus on hunger, working with local food banks to increase access to food. After having some initial success in our local communities, we began looking to find ways to address hunger on a broader statewide and national basis.

Working with one of my senior executives responsible for government relations and advocacy, we decided to start this initiative quietly. At the time, there weren't many health care organizations nationally focused on nonclinical aspects of health and well-being, and in fact, this is still a concept that is foreign to many in the health care industry.

Initially, even though we recognized that what we were doing had tremendous potential and was a great story to tell, we decided to build public momentum for this initiative slowly. We kept saying to each other, "Don't tell anybody yet. Let's keep it to ourselves for now." I read recently that if you do something innovative, you should expect to be misunderstood for years! I agree completely with that.

It was always a challenge for everyone to stay humble. When you look at the Beatitudes, the values Christ talked about are very consistent with what we are doing with the social determinants of health. Like Christ's example, there was no need to be overt about what we were doing. Servant leadership does not require that you be overt. You don't have to say you are a Christian; you just show it through your actions. Not everyone will agree with that, but I think that is really true for most Christians.

We were thoughtful about how we communicated about social determinants with our various critical audiences, like board members, physicians and clinical staff, our employees, community leaders, and the community at large. The objective was to bring others along slowly, because at the time, this was a fairly radical way for an organization to use its resources.

We were able to win over our key audiences about the importance of engaging with our communities, not only because it was the right thing to do for our community but also because it enhanced patient outcomes and resulted in health care cost reductions. And slowly, we began to be more overt with how we communicated to the public at large.

Thirteen-plus years later, addressing social determinants of health is totally integrated into our mission and vision. It is part of long-term strategic plan that touches every aspect of our business. For example, the move of our corporate employees and headquarters from the suburbs to the core of what had been a decimated downtown was influenced by the need to bring economic development back to the downtown of an ailing city. It was a move that brought more than ten thousand employees located in various locations in the city to the downtown. We totally renovated a vacant steam plant that was over a hundred years old and vacant for the last thirty years to serve as one of the buildings to house our employees. It would have been less expensive to build a new facility in the suburbs, but it meant more for the community as a whole for us to be downtown.

Because health begins where people live, thanks to the generosity of a donor, we were able to establish a Neighborhood Promise, which is an initiative that focuses on neighborhood revitalization. As part of this, we established an inner-city, full-service grocery store in an area that was previously a food desert and provided financial coaching, job training, and community classes.

On a national level, along with the AARP Foundation, we established the Root Cause Coalition, which is now a network of seventy-plus organizations across the country working to reverse and end the systemic root causes of health inequities for individuals and communities.

Like many major nonprofits, we acted as an an anchor institution in the communities we serve. Anchor institutions are typically large, often nonprofit organizations that are rooted or anchored in their communities— so that usually includes universities, health systems or medical centers, or other large companies in any community that are committed to economic development and community transformation. As an anchor institution in the communities we served, we were committed to looking beyond a singular focus on clinical and financial success. We focused on things that have the most significant impact on people's health and well-being. That means focusing on things like housing, income, poverty, safety, education, and health behaviors. And that means doing things like establishing a grocery store in a food desert in a central city location, investments in preserving affordable housing, and partnering with other organizations to reinvest in building up communities.

Moving from Awareness to Advocacy and Then to Action

How do you move them from awareness to advocacy to action? It took years for us to move our critical audience to bring them along relative to social determinants.

Health care is a mess. It is not the health care model you would set up today if you were starting from scratch. I go to meetings and hear how much money organizations are making. And yet health care is largely unaffordable. It is the number one cause of personal bankruptcy. It is something that is so wrong, and we have a responsibility to change it. But creating real momentum and change sometimes feels achingly slow.

The COVID pandemic really impacted people of color and the most vulnerable in our society in a disproportionate fashion. Yet that didn't really motivate policy makers to want to find a path to a new model. The concept of social determinants of health is so foreign to so many people. It is still a kind of inside-the-Beltway conversation. But we keep working at it. For whatever reason, it still hasn't made its way into the general population's DNA. Health care is such a behemoth, policy makers are reluctant to really take it on and get to the root causes of health and well-being.

Humility, Patience, and Persistence

Humility is a key characteristic of a Christian as a servant leader, but it does not mean that you are cowering. One of the best pieces of advice I got during my career was from a mentor at a health system in western Michigan. He took me aside and said I needed to get myself in a position, mentally and spiritually as well as financially, where I didn't need the job. His point was to always be in a position do what's right. And you can't be worried about feeling that you are making decisions to make people happy. At times, you need to put yourself in a position where you can make decisions and not be concerned about disagreeing with others. That will always resolve itself. But having that approach allows you to have pure motivations and to make sure your decisions are sound, because you are not worried about the financial impact of your job or that someone is going to be upset with you for the decisions you made. Taking this approach helps ensure you are more likely to do what is right.

John Woolman was an American Quaker who lived during the mideighteenth century.[5] Many eighteenth-century American Quakers were affluent, conservative slaveholders. Woolman almost singlehandedly rid the Quaker Society of Friends of slaves and spent most of his adult life devoted to ridding the society of this practice. By 1770, well before the Civil War, he had accomplished his goal. He was passionate about what he was doing, and he was compassionate in how he helped people think through the issue of slavery. He achieved his mission not by yelling loudly or through intimidation but through clear, gentle, persistent persuasion. He asked questions that helped his fellow Quakers understand what owning slaves does to an individual as a moral person and what kind of legacy that would leave for the next generation of Quakers.

The concept of quiet, persistent persuasion is all too often the opposite of what we see so-called leaders do today. The approach is to intimidate, with the idea that the person who yells the loudest will succeed. This is not the example of Christ's leadership, and in the long term, that bullying leadership approach will fail.

Woolman, as a peacemaker, was able to be completely effective with the Quaker society. He offered clear, gentle persuasion. So Christian leaders should think about their role: instead of loudly debating, think about giving compassion, showing mercy, and having a pureness of heart.

You can create urgency and stay humble. You can create that sense of urgency through your own action and by asking questions. For example, as part of the social determinant of health initiative at my organization, we have been working with state and national leaders in Congress to establish a national commission to create a new model of health care that provides comprehensive access to care, increases resources for primary care, mental health, and public health, and addresses the social determinants of health and health disparities in our country. We have been at it for six years. Each year, we get a little closer. And it will happen. Through patience, persistence, and our actions.

This approach to leadership takes a great deal of discipline. And it can take time to accomplish goals. You will encounter ego-driven people who are focused on nothing but immediate self-gratification, and you will have to continue to adjust and plug away at achieving your goals.

We worry way too much how popular we are and how many material possessions we have. Better to have the discipline to be a humble soldier for Christ (2 Timothy 2:3–4). Sometimes you see that exemplified with pastors of small congregations. Their humbled service is perhaps not as valued as those pastors of megachurches, and that is a shame. With the pandemic, we saw the humble service of those in health care along with all the first responders, more visible as the humble servants that they are, in a very real way putting others before themselves. But it will be interesting to see how people react to these first responders as the pandemic becomes an endemic and winds down some. Will people still appreciate the humble service that these people provide? I hope so.

Ultimately, servant leaders will not be judged by how much we have done in life for others but by how much we could have done. I look at people who have great financial success and resource wealth, and they could really help our communities move forward. Some do, but some do not. And that is fine, but the more people take time to think about devoting even a small percentage of the resources they have to improving individual and community health and well-being, think of the impact that could be made.

Be Spiritually Bankrupt

You read a lot about the dangers of leadership where you begin to think that you are entitled to things or deserve things. The point here is to keep yourself lowly in your own eyes. It is about your motivation. Is it to receive recognition? Power? It is not about what you deserve. Keep yourself honest. I was a pretty average student; I got better as I got older. I came from a financially poor household. If you had asked my former teachers in grade school who was going to succeed, it wasn't me. So remember your humble beginnings. Be spiritually bankrupt before God.

A Beatitude is a talent bestowed, a talent given. And when you think about that, you think about how important it is to not waste that blessing. You have no ability to work to make up for the debt you have to God. He saved you. You are poor spiritually, financially, and mentally and really in everything you have. You are poor in all these aspects without God. I am lost without Christ and God. If you are broke and in poverty, that is one thing. But if you are poor in spirit, it is a recognition of who you are as a person.

Beatitudes: Applying the Values to Servant Leadership

In the last chapter, we talked about how living and applying the Beatitudes was a key value of Christ and his leadership example. You can live the Beatitudes in your work life even though you may not be in a position to call them Christian.

At my organization, our approach to addressing social determinants and health inequities is an example of using a leadership position to be able to make an impact in the community in ways that are highly Christian, but we just don't call them that. That is acting Christian in day-to-day leading.

The Beatitudes are so contrary to things you might think about when you think about business. Servant leadership is a great buzz word, and it rolls off the tongue smoothly. But those are the sorts of things where you can lay it out. It is all right there.

You have to be careful how you frame change in areas like the social determinants. Some people might think you are using your role in a company to do your Christian work. But clearly it is who you are and what motivates you in life. But it is also the right thing to do and makes sense from a business and clinical standpoint as well as from a faith-based perspective.

The Discipline of Servant Leadership

While the Beatitudes may feel comforting, Jesus makes it clear to his disciples that living the Beatitudes is hard work and requires considerable discipline, as in Matthew 10:38 and Matthew 16:24. His followers must "deny themselves and take up their cross and follow me." In this way, the cross represents both a narrow path and love. He is clear in telling the disciples that because of Christ and what he stood for, people will persecute them.

He instructs the disciples that he has not come to abolish the law of the prophets but to fulfill them, and that to be called to the kingdom of heaven, they must practice and teach these commands. In Matthew 5:17–20, Christ tells them in no uncertain terms that their righteousness must surpasses that of the Pharisees and the teachers of the law.

But as he continues to instruct, Jesus does reframe what the Pharisees and scribes are saying in a series of directives that begin with "You have heard that … But I tell you …" related to murder, adultery, divorce, oaths, and the concept of an "eye for and eye" (Matthew 38–48). He ends this series with a statement about love for your enemies. "You have heard … love your neighbor and hate your enemy. But I tell you, do not resist an evil person. If anyone slaps you on the right cheek, turn to them the other cheek also."

This all means you have to have great discipline. Matthew 7:13–14 is clear: "Enter through the narrow gate. For wide is the gate and broad is the road that leads to destruction, and many enter through it. But small is the gate and narrow the road that leads to life, and only a few find it."

Maintaining Emotional Health as a Disciple

In his book *Emotionally Healthy Discipleship: Moving from Shallow Christianity to Deep Transformation*, Peter Scazzero provides some good insight into what it means to have an emotionally healthy discipleship.[6] He offers guidelines to help determine how the values of the Western culture have compromised the call of Jesus to deny ourselves and follow him, provides clear criteria to measure maturity by how we grow in our ability to love others, and embraces weakness and vulnerability as a way to offer God's love to the world. We have to think about how faith fits in with our purpose in life and how that fits into our approach to mental health. Faith can be an incredible support or undergirding to how you live your life. Mental health, perspective, confidence, comfort, being able to understand and use the talents you have—they all can be supported through faith and embraced as a servant leader.

Have Faith as a Servant Leader

There is always a balance. Do you aspire to be in a leadership position for its prestige and power, or is a matter of putting yourself in a position where you can have an impact on someone's life? I was talking to one of my fellow executives the other day, and she was saying that my faith has served me well in my career. I was surprised by the comment, but it was true! It grounds you in a way that you don't overact to situations and challenges. Some might wish that I got more excited. It is not that you don't care when a crisis arises, but because you are connected to your career and profession in a different way, it offers you a calmness that might not otherwise be there. Your faith gives you confidence. Christ expresses this concept in a number of ways throughout the Gospels. For example, while at sea, Christ calms the waters during a rough storm and tells his disciples to "have faith" as the waters calm. He feeds thousands of people with what seems to be a very limited food supply. God will provide.

Some people in our organization get all cranked up when the news media does not cover our organization in way that we think is fair. And they wonder why I don't get more upset. We still are going to move forward and do the right thing. You have to write your own story. Each of our stories is distinct. You can't live other people's life. Follow your story. Appreciate what is happening and have confidence. Your faith and what you believe are prime in helping you succeed in life. The idea is to lean on Christ and not your own understanding. It's like resting a hand on Christ's shoulder as you navigate the narrow path of life.

The Seeming Inconsistency of the "I Am" Statements

Throughout the Gospel according to John, there are a series of statements that begin with "I am" that are powerful statements. As a leader, when you first read these, you might think it a little odd, because it seems to leave an impression that Christ is not humble. But when you understand the context of the entire chapter, these statements provide strong examples of Christ's servant leadership approach.

Below in *italics* is the start of each "I am" statement. The second extension of the statement is intended to help explain how the statement might relate to us as servant leaders.

I am the good shepherd (John 10:11) ...

This chapter is the essence of servant leadership. Christ talks about knowing his sheep, how the sheep know him, and how he would lay down his life for his sheep. But it is not just his sheep. He has other sheep that are not his, but he is willing to listen to them and bring them along also.

I am the bread of life (John 6:35) ...

In this chapter of John, Jesus has just finished feeding the five thousand. But if we think metaphorically about Jesus as the substance of leadership, we might improve as servant leaders.

I am the light of the world (John 8:12) ...

This chapter in John is about the woman caught in adultery. The Pharisees' brand of justice is to stone the woman. Jesus does not condemn the woman; rather, he tells her to "Go now and leave your life of sin." He does not judge her by human standards. So, in this way, Jesus has provided an example of how a servant leader can find justice in in this world.

I am the way (John 14:6) ...

In this chapter, Jesus is comforting his disciples. Through him, the disciples will find truth.

When you think about it, these "I am" statements can be used as a tool to check secular and church leaders. If you hear from a megachurch pastor or some Ivy League MBA who is focused only on numbers, for example, as a Christian leader, you reject that idea.

To Achieve Greatness, First Be a Servant

At the Last Supper, an argument broke out among Christ's disciples to determine who was the greatest, jockeying for position to see who would sit at his right hand or his left hand. Christ shut down this debate by saying that the first will be last.

As humans, the sons of Zebedee see everything that Christ has done and how he has accomplished it through the example of servant leadership. The next minute, they are arguing about who is the greatest, which is totally contrary to what Christ taught and how he led. You think, *You have been traveling with this humble man and have witnessed the things he has done, and you are arguing about who is the greatest and will sit on the right or left of Jesus.*

The concept of servant leadership that comes out of the Sermon on the Mount and the Beatitudes really flipped the script on how leaders thought about the nature of things. Jesus focused on the poor in spirit, the mourners, the meek, the merciful, the pure in heart, the peacemakers. In many ways, that is as new today as it was back in the time of Christ. It is not the way Wall Street influencers necessarily preach, and these are not considered the attributes of a strong leaders. Christian leaders at times have ignored these views. That is why we must always keep these values and concepts in mind moving forward.

To that end, Christ was not only a servant leader; he was also leader of change who refined and redefined the laws of the times, which takes us to our next chapter.

NINE

LEADING CHANGE

When talking to people about my leadership approach, I often focus on three key principles—that a leader needs to create a sense of urgency, tell people thank you, and always remind people that everything will turn out all right.

The foundation for these concepts come from John Kotter, who wrote the book *Leading Change* in 1996, which was selected by *Time* magazine in 2011 as one the twenty-five most influential business books ever written.[1] Words like "visionary guide," "more relevant than ever," and "practical toolkit," are all used to describe his work.

Through Kotter's eight-step process, the company he formed helps companies transform their organizations and their leaders and helps teach others how to implement their change process. And they have been very successful over the years in doing this.

Yet what was striking to me was that as I looked at the example of Christ's life and his leadership approach, he was already a clear example of these best-selling leadership concepts. Undoubtedly, Jesus Christ led the greatest change in history. The impact of this poor carpenter in his three-year ministry is unfathomable.

In his book, Yale historian Jeroslav Pelikan wrote that "Regardless of what anyone may personally think or believe about him, Jesus of Nazareth has been the dominant figure in the history of Western culture for almost 20 centuries."[2] During his time, his leadership resulted in dramatic change in society that we are still feeling today.

The evidence is everywhere. During Christ's time, children were treated horribly, especially if you were the wrong gender—and you might be left to die or sold into slavery. Jesus's leadership and teaching brought light to these issues and helped end these practices. In Mark 10:14, he says to the people, "Let the little children come to me, and do not hinder them, for the kingdom of God belongs to such as these." His compassion for those most in need transcended the laws of his time; for example, his compassion for lepers led to the development of institutions to treat them, and in a sense, it led to the beginning of the modern-day hospital. Cathedrals began also to function as a place to care for the sick and poor. There was no sense of humility in the world Christ lived in; his washing the feet of servants set the leadership example that humility should be an admired virtue. During his time, it was a considered a virtue to crush your enemies; Jesus helped to raise up the importance of forgiveness to those who would do you harm. And he was a vocal champion and activist for humanitarian reform for women, slaves, and the most fragile in society, which angered those in positions of power.

To help illustrate the connection between Christ's leadership style and contemporary experts who have created models for leading change, what follows is a little bit of a deep dive into a contemporary secular concept in leading change compared to Christ's leadership example. Throughout this chapter, we will provide each step in John Kotter's process and then show how Christ lived the concept thousands of years ago. In addition, I will offer a few examples of how we implement these processes for change at my organization. You can decide if the style reflects Christ's leadership approach or Kotter's eight-step process.

Kotter's Eight-Stage Process of Creating Major Change versus Jesus's Process of Creating Major Change

Jesus's Change Process	Kotter's Eight-Stage Process	Relevant Bible Verse(s)
Took on status quo; identified failed leadership; reinterpreted and extended the Torah (while still seeking to fulfill the Torah); acted in counterintuitive ways; worked on Sabbath; reshaped the exercise of piety; almsgiving, prayer, fasting	Establishing a sense of urgency	Luke 10:3–4, 10:9 Mark 11:15–18 Matthew 5:17–40 Luke 20:27–40 (interpretation of burning bush story) Matthew 6:1–18 Mark 11:27–33
Identified and brought in the disciples and apostles; built coalition among those who were in need; extended and reinterpreted the Torah; established and sent out the seventy-two	Creating a guiding coalition	Luke 6:12–49 Luke 10
Identified mission and values; identified wanted behaviors (the Great Commandment; the Beatitudes); identified unwanted behaviors (the woes); articulated a vision of being fishers of men, making disciples of all the nations	Developing a vision and strategy	Mission: Matthew 6:33; Vision: Matthew 28:16–20 Values: Matthew 22:3–39; 10–12; 15–17; 3–12; 6:19–?) Mark 12:29–34 Luke 6:27–36
Communication through disciples/ apostles sending out messengers; Gospels; sermons; letters; parables; modeled change; asking questions; defining reality; providing instructions	Communicating the change vision	Matthew 1:1–42 Matthew 28:18–20 Luke 9:52

Sent disciples out and empowered them to achieve the Great Commission; the power of prayer	Empowering broad-based action	Matthew 10 Luke 10–16 Mark 6:7–13
Performed miracles	Generating short-term wins	Mark 1:29–34, 40–42
Repeatedly in Acts, the ongoing success of the church's mission is stressed in summaries that mark its progress: Christians succeed not only in being faithful disciples themselves but also in "turning the world upside down" in having a transforming effect on society. Numerous stories present the church as triumphant over all forms of evil, wiping out poverty, healing diseases.	Consolidation gains and producing more change	Acts: 1:14; 2:41; 4:4; 5:14; 6:7; 9:31; 11:21, 24; 12:24; 14:1; 16:5; 19:20; 28:30–31 Acts 17:6 Acts 4:32–37 Acts 5:12–16 Luke 10:17–18
Disciples/apostles get out the word; creation of the New Testament, including the four Gospels; prioritizing actions	Anchoring new approaches in the culture	Matthew 6

As you look at this comparison, I ask you, who led the greatest change in the history of this world? Jesus Christ! John Kotter needs to pay some royalties to the church! Just kidding, of course, but you get the idea. The fundamentals of change leadership can be perfectly seen through the example of Christ's leadership.

1. Establishing a Sense of Urgency

Christ understood the need to create a sense of urgency among his followers because he recognized he had only a limited time on earth. He achieved that urgency in multiple ways.

Christ created urgency by *challenging the status quo*. This is entirely natural in many ways because Christ came from humble beginnings. He didn't belong to the upper class or those in power. He came from a family that would have been considered lower class during those times. It was a natural extension for him to want to help the lowly and give the common person hope.

It is a really interesting dynamic between the Beatitudes and then what he did taking on the organized church. At times, Christ went out of his way to challenge authority figures. He made a choice to not back down. He took a different approach with his disciples but in ways that still created urgency. He told Peter, "You are the rock that I am going to build my church around." Next, he chastised him for not listening after he told them three times he was going to die. When he was resurrected, he reassured them that everything was going to be all right. This approach built a natural tension and a sense of urgency.

Christ *provided inspiration* as a leader in so many ways. When he called the fishermen to be disciples, he told them he would make them fishers of men. He told them that they were going to do something they had never done before. They were going to change the world. They didn't always understand what he was telling them, but in this aspirational way, he called them to this vision, way beyond their imagination. To a point, that is what we need to do as leaders. He did it differently with people, relative to their individual context. He was confrontational with religious authorities; for those who were around him, he counseled, he mentored, he called them on the carpet, he lifted them up. For the poorest of the poor, he was completely meek and met them where they were at.

Christ tried to facilitate change on a global, local, and personal level. Kotter talks about things in terms of an overall organizational level. Christ goes beyond that.

The Gospels are the framework for life. Every year, I try to read through the New Testament and particularly the Gospels. Over the last couple of years, I have tried to read or listen to the Gospels every day, and it acts as a framework and a life guide that provides reassurance. As a Christian, you are constantly looking to change, to be better, to do more to help others.

The Gospels are essentially a way of prioritizing and organizing your life. It is interesting how Christ focused on the Beatitudes and the Great

Commandment, when he could have focused on a lot of other things. Some of it reflects the times and who he was preaching to. For me, the Beatitudes (blessed are the poor in spirit, those who mourn, the meek, those who thirst for righteousness, the merciful, the pure in heart, the peacemakers, and those who are persecuted because of righteousness) act like a looped tape that runs through the back of my mind all the time, an infinite reel running through my head at all times every day while focusing on mission, values, change, and change principles. Reading the Beatitudes every couple of days helps embed that loop into your thinking.

Christ *modeled behavior.* At times, he was incredibly humble; at times, he avoided crowds; at times, he was a true servant leader who washed feet; and at times, he was healing and caring for people. He engaged children, women, and all races. He was truly the type of person we all want to be.

One of the things Christ did in in creating a sense of urgency was that *he forced choices.* In Luke 12:51–52, Jesus says, "Do you think I came to bring peace on earth? No …" When you create urgency, you create some divisions. Either you believe or you don't. Either you have faith or you don't. Either you accept Christ or you don't. That may seem a little harsh at times. That is exactly what it is about. So sometimes we are forced to choose, and not choosing is a choice. As leaders, that is sometimes what we must do—force a choice.

Achieving balance and maintaining a calm environment as you create urgency is a challenge.

When you are creating urgency, there will be times when you worry that you might be burning people out and that you need to let your foot off the pedal. How do you strike that risk/reward balance when creating urgency? There is an incredible thrill of innovation. Truthfully, I am kind of an innovation junky, so I am probably one of the worst offenders of driving forward. I know that can be frustrating at times. One financial adviser friend commented to a group that I always start with "yes," and people earn a "no," which he noted was just the opposite of so many other people. That's a blessing, I think; others would call it a curse. Sometimes you do need to pull back and say, "Thank you. You are doing great." On the other hand, if you look at it from a broader contextual perspective, it is more about creating an environment and culture for innovation.

Every major company probably should have about thirty significant projects going on at any one time. Some of those projects are at a beginning stage, while others are more fully developed to the point where you think they are going to happen. You try to create this environment where you constantly have this innovative churn of ideas and an atmosphere of growth. But the balance there is that you have to be careful that thirty doesn't become one hundred projects and that you don't overwhelm people.

Even though Christ knew his time on earth was limited and that he had an incredible mission to accomplish in a brief timeline, he took breaks. There are many passages where he escapes. Prayer really helped to ground him. He got away from the crowd and went to the mountains to pray. He could've burned his disciples out going from place to place. But he had a pace that worked and serves as an example of how we can balance the need to constantly grow with the caution to not overwhelm.

Mark Granovetter is an American sociologist and professor at Stanford University who published an influential essay in 1973 called "The Strength of Weak Ties," with more than fifty thousand citations according to Google Scholar.[3] The general idea of the paper is that, often in life, we connect with people who agree with us, people with whom we have easy and strong ties. As a result, ideas in that group tend to be redundant. Because of this, Granovetter argues that people with whom you have weak ties may provide you more innovative ideas, specifically because they don't have strong ties to or with you. It is seemingly inconsistent perhaps, but Granovetter provided evidence that this was the case.

Jesus Christ also was *at times seemingly inconsistent in his leadership style,* perhaps most eloquently illustrated as he assembled the twelve disciples. You talk about the strength of weak ties. Here is a nonpolitician carpenter who later in life knit together this fabric of disciples who were not powerful to carry his message. This is completely opposite of the ruling class at the time, the Romans, who demanded loyalty, or the church. This goes against the grain of all times.

He did things that were inconsistent with the rules of the day, like working on the Sabbath, or other things in the scriptures that were added on by the rulers of the day. He helped people focus on what was important.

In its early days, our focus on the social determinants of health certainly seemed incongruent with our core mission to some board members, leaders, employees, leaders in our communities, and even those looking at our initiatives within the health care arena. Everything in health care was, and more often than not continues to be, focused on the clinical and the financial. Focusing on issues outside the four walls of a hospital or a physician's office to address seemed to be out of our lane for many. But the more we began to look at issues like food access and insecurity, housing, poverty and financial stability, personal safety, community development, and other factors, it became increasingly clear that those issues had greater impact on long-term health and well-being than clinical factors.

Jesus wanted to help ensure the God's laws would be fulfilled; in that way, Jesus declared that he came not to abolish the law but to fulfill it (Matthew 5:17). *But he also wanted to modify, change, or even ignore human-made laws.* In some cases, he rigorously supported laws, and in other cases, he told people to ignore laws and to follow the commandments of Christ.

He took some laws head-on. For example, he stated that working and healing the sick on the Sabbath (which was forbidden) was allowed because it was the right thing to do (Matthew 12:12).

The Great Commandments (love God with all your heart, soul, and mind, and love your neighbor as yourself) and the golden rule (do unto others as you would want to be treated) are just two of the more famous modifications Jesus made to the laws. These are changes to the law that focused on what God intended as opposed to what man-made laws permit or prohibit.

As he created urgency, *Christ challenged authority figures.* He didn't start his ministry until he was thirty years old. He worked hard, he studied, he knew the law, he knew scripture, he knew religion, and he had some practical experience as a carpenter. When he started speaking out and began his ministry, he was really well prepared. He did it in a creative, inspirational way.

Christ came along and freed us from a lot of strict human laws that people in power had created so they could stay in power. He gave us new marching orders. The Old Testament is excellent in giving us historical context, but that is why the focus on Christ's life and leadership is so important, because when you look at the things he said and did, he railed against those in positions of authority who abused power and had the wrong motivation in life.

It is important to seek deeper meaning. You can find meaning in a number of different ways: you can take a rigid, dogmatic approach, or you can take a strict theological approach. And yet I think a lot of finding the deeper meaning is in how you apply it to your life. What is the meaning in my life? What can I glean from Christ that would help me define my life, my purpose, my calling in life, the way I want to treat people? That is how you can use Christ's example as a guide for your life and as a leader.

The reality of Christ's day was one of an organized, powerful, and corrupt religious hierarchy. Then Christ came in and recruited twelve people who were not anything like the leaders of the day. He ministered to the poor, the disabled, those who had all kind of needs, and he hung out with Samaritan women. He took his message to the masses. Christ redefined and refined reality and turned everything on its head, which is kind of happening today.

Christ was good at *taking on the authorities but avoiding traps* they set for him. When the Pharisees were accusing a woman caught in adultery, they were less concerned about punishing the woman than they were in trying to trap Jesus into saying something inappropriate. Jesus avoided the trap, but as he responded, he was writing something on the ground with his finger. We don't know what he actually wrote, but many feel he was writing down the names of those who were ready to throw stones at this woman with a list of their sins. He knew of their hypocrisy. When Jesus called out that those with no sin could throw the first stone, the leaders quickly realized that the trap didn't work, and they all dropped their stones and walked away.

2. Creating a Guiding Coalition

As you create urgency, you need to begin to assemble a leadership team to carry out the mission. Christ did that, but his coalition was a ragtag group. They were uneducated fishermen, tax collectors, people in poverty. It was a group of people who in his time you would never pick to be leaders if you were trying to change the world, yet he picked them. He really offered things to people who had little or nothing in life, and that was really who he came for.

He had his twelve disciples as his inner circle, and he trained them. But in addition to this, he embraced a larger group to facilitate the message and facilitate change. When we started our work on social determinants, we started in small steps with a small group of people who were passionate about it, and we didn't talk about it loudly, but once we had a vision and success, we increasingly cast out a wider and wider net. Even now, more than eleven years later and with some significant successes, we keep thinking about creating more urgency. We would have hoped that more people and organizations would have been looking at social determinants and how to develop programs in their communities, and clearly, because of the way health care works, they are not nearly as focused as we would have hoped. The work continues, and we need to create more urgency. Now we are trying to help people see what success looks like and why addressing these health disparities is so critically important.

I think that is that same for Christ. Jesus became more well known as his miracles brought him more attention and the word continued to spread, and the result was that the momentum just continued to grow and spread. He had a coalition of people he kept close, and he cast the vision and reinforced it. As he did this, he was implementing this vision.

The disciples had issues. They were petty at times and argued about who was the greatest (Luke 9:46, 22:24). They used their authority to exclude others (Luke 19:15–16). At times, they were men who seemed to have little faith (Matthew 8:26) or no faith at all (Mark 4:40). They may actually have seemed to be way too confident and needed to learn how to use their resources to have a positive impact. We will discuss this in much greater detail in the next chapter. But Christ brought them together, and they became an extremely effective team in spreading his word.

3. Developing a Vision and Strategy

As we talked about in the previous chapter, Christ had a powerful mission and values that guided him throughout his time and gave the disciples the foundation needed to carry out the mission after his death. Ultimately, the mission, vision, and values are all about your purpose. And Christ understood his purpose better than anyone. From a Christian leader standpoint, data tells us that if, as a leader, you help people understand their personal purpose and come to grips with that, they will be more supportive of the organizational purpose and be more engaged. Christ did this by modeling behavior and helping the disciples understand him and by creating an environment where they could succeed.

The miracles were a critical component to developing and implementing the vision and mission. Among other things, the miracles illustrated the power of his ministry and how it would be marked by helping others and preaching with authority in close interactions with people. The miracles connected his message with action. He didn't do miracles for himself. He did miracles to illustrate to others who he was, what he was about, what his mission was, and what success looked like. In talking to Thomas after his resurrection, Jesus said, "Because you have seen me, you have believed; blessed are those who have not seen and yet believed" (John 20:29). And they had just believed the message, so that was pretty powerful.

There are times Jesus established *a vision of a world turned upside down*. In Acts 17:6, there is a description of the faithful disciples turning the world upside down and being successful in doing so. It is a great descriptor— everything that the world tells us we need to consider with a kind of upside-down view. Christ leading change is radically different from any human kingdom. Even when he was baptized by John the Baptist, he stood in line and didn't expect any royal treatment. He lived in an obscure city. What Christ did in many ways was completely the opposite of what the leaders of his day thought, and even opposite of what leaders today think. We have to think of Christian leadership as opposite to that of traditional leaders and world leadership.

Recently, like many other organizations throughout the United States, my organization announced that it was forming a new regional lesbian, gay, bisexual, transgender, queer and/or questioning, intersex, and asexual patient-family advisory group. The intent is to get feedback from these constituents so that we can do a better job of providing care and meeting the needs of people, no matter what their sexual orientation might be.

Interestingly, I have not gotten any blowback from this from the Christian community. I got a lot of negative feedback from the Christian community regarding issues related to our organization's stand on abortions and that we would accept patients from clinics who conducted abortions, as well as issues related to stem cell research. But so far, I have not gotten negative feedback on the formation of this advisory group. Perhaps it is because I keep harping that we take care of everyone who walks through our door, and we are going to treat people with dignity and respect no matter who they are or what they believe. I know a business owner who was in the process of recruiting a new leader to be on a diversity, equity, inclusion group, until he said, "I don't get this race stuff. I am not sure I buy into it." Those sorts of things are upsetting. We can't judge. Christ accepted everyone. He railed against those who were convoluting the Christian faith.

In addition to taking on the status quo and false leaders, *Christ also reframed and extended the scriptures.* In the Sermon on the Mount, there is a series of statements where Christ says, "You may have heard this," and then he reframes the statement by adding "but this …" That is something we do every day as leaders. That concept of reframing and extending the narrative is something we try to do constantly and is at the core of how the company continues to evolve.

Our organization, which had its origins as a hospital system, is now calling itself a "health and well-being" company; we used to call ourselves an integrated delivery system; and now we talk about one of our goals to achieve a national, consumer-facing concierge model for people to navigate their health and well-being is an extension of our work. It is part of "What are we going to do next? What's the next major goal? How do we evolve? And evolution for us is this national health and well-being model. That is what leaders do. You help people and organizations evolve. And that was what Christ was trying to do. He was on a limited timeframe. Some of the things he was able to do gently; to accomplish other things, he had to be less gentle.

4. Communicating the Change Vision

We will talk about how Christ communicated his mission in the chapter on communication and cultivating relationships. But suffice it to say that how people got the word out during Christ's time was in many ways much more challenging than communicating to mass populations in today's high-tech environment. And yet Christ was extremely effective and strategic at accomplishing the goal of communicating the change vision and mission. He relied on his disciples and apostles to serve as extensions of his word. He waded into very public events and discourses wherever he traveled. He was very strategic about where he went and what settings he was in to maximize his communication. There were times when he calmly taught and then times when he was outwardly aggressive, like when he overturned the tables of the money changers, which sent a strong message to people. He also found time for reflection when he prayed. He modeled change in many ways. And he communicated through his sermons and, after his death, through the Gospels.

Through communications, he helped define reality. The Beatitudes and Sermon on the Mount provided instructions to his disciples and others about how to implement his mission.

He also was a great storyteller. As he established change, he spoke to the people at their level. He, more than anyone, told stories and parables, which were a revolutionary communication technique in his time and gave people something to act on.

The ability to convey a mission and vision is essential for today's Christian leader. We need to take complex issues and make them simple. That was what Christ did as a leader. The parables simplified Christ's message in many ways and were an innovative and effective way to reach audiences.

Christ was a master at challenging people by asking questions. The leaders of the time would ask questions, and he would often respond with a question that frustrated the Pharisees and other leaders. He often challenged his disciples with questions to get them to think deeply about issues. The art of asking questions is essential for leaders today. It can help define issues.

I am often amazed in meetings when people are presenting ideas and strategies and are more worried about what they are going to say than asking questions and listening; as a result, they often jump to wrong conclusions. You have to slow things down and help people think through processes, and you can do that by asking questions. Once you start to ask questions, you often have a completely different discussion than where you started. It seems like common sense, but it doesn't happen as much as you think.

When I am reviewing materials during a presentation, I try to write my questions in the margins. My goal is to wait toward the end of the dialogue, see what others ask, and then I ask questions. A few people are really good at asking bigger, broader questions when having a strategic discussion. I remember one time at a board meeting, we were having a great discussion about an issue, and one of the board members asked a very specific question about one particular detail of the plan we were discussing. Micromanagement to the max. And I thought, *That is what you got out of that?* But this person was an engineer, and his mind went to specific details in how things worked, so that probably explained his focused question.

As storytelling devices, the Sermon on the Mount and the parables helped to raise questions about values and provided instructions on how to frame up your life. The Sermon is really all about how we should prioritize our life. It provides both a foundation and a focus.

As a leader, you begin to think about organizational change, and some days it is easier than others. But as a leader, you are always thinking about what the next thing is, what the next step is. How can we make the organization better? Where does that lead us next? This helps not only with the organization but also with the environment.

Addressing the social determinants really made our leadership and board members consider a broader view of health and well-being, and it made sense for us to look at how we care for people and our communities. But as you do that, you have to remain flexible. You start to think about the steps that will take you to point A, to where you would like to be, and you have to be realistic while creating urgency. If there are ten steps in the process, you might not be able to get from one through ten in the first year, but you can accomplish one through four, so that becomes your focus. This means that as you are implementing the mission, you are always trying to make changes and refocus the organization. As you do this, you have to make sure there is clarity of purpose, clarity of expectations, and clarity of who is in charge of what. And then you go back and review each year to determine if you are in a better place than you were a year ago and ask tough questions.

When you think about Christ as a leader of change, sometimes you might hear someone say, "WWJD," which stands for "What would Jesus do?" That may not be the right question or statement. A better question to ask might be "What *did* Jesus do?" Because we should focus on his actual behaviors. It is more action oriented and more historically accurate. You can see how he acted, how he reacted. He had at the time what was a radical religion. He was calling people to absolute faith. He over changed the money changers. That is not what we do anymore. We feel we have to be overly cautious and not criticize. *Words do matter, but look at actions first.*

5. Empowering Broad-Based Actions

When you look Christ telling his disciples, "Go and make ye disciples of all nations," that is a pretty broad-based action. The first thing he said was, "Go."

It created urgency and action. And he was very clear on his goal to create disciples from all nations. He was a person of passion and of action.

In Revelation 3:15–16, Jesus talks about preferring people who are hot or cold but not lukewarm. He wanted people who were passionate one way or another. Christ realized that those who just kind of want to hang around, who are lukewarm, are sometimes harder to move to action. As a leader, the people who don't take a position are sometimes the most challenging in empowering action. Sadly enough, some people survive their entire careers that way.

Prayer (which we talk more about in the chapter on perspective) is also an incredible tool in empowering action. Prayer can be a calming, centering activity that can help solidify a feeling of hope, belief, and commitment in individuals. In Philippians 4:6–7, we are told that with prayer and petition, you can bring your requests to God and that the peace of God that transcends all understanding will guard your heart and mind in Christ Jesus. When you think of verses like that, prayer can be incredibly important in helping provide comfort and reduce anxieties, which in turn allows people to take action. The idea of having requests made empowers you emotionally, physically, and emotionally.

I haven't done this my entire life, but over the last year or so, I try to pray more on my knees. Even for a few minutes. I have to admit that is a transformational feeling. I don't do it for fifteen minutes, but even a few minutes gives me a peace and is very powerful. I wish I had done it more my whole life!

As a Christian leader, sometimes you have to empower broad-based action, and you have to be persistent about achieving the action. We had a meeting recently with representatives on the Ways and Means Committee. And in my mind, I was thinking, *Can we just stop talking about all these issues and just do something about these inequities?* We've known about the impact of social determinants of health and health disparities for decades. We need to stop just offering lip service. Infant and maternal mortality is not a new issue. We have done some things. But all too often, we just have discussions, and there are not actions. You can't just help a baby be born. Your job is now to help this child thrive and have the opportunities you would want. We have to examine what we are doing. In some very quick ways, you could start to make positive change. There could be an industry standard that all health care organizations nationally are responsible for screening for the social determinants of health and have a coordinated plan for interventions, and we are going to hold you accountable for that. As Christian leaders, these are some things we can do to impact people's live in a very real and measurable way.

Early in my career, I had the good fortune of having a really good mentor. He was really good at asking questions. He would examine a business plan and ask lots and lots of questions. When I did business plans for him, he would grill me on my assumptions. I was kidding with him once that one day I would do a business plan for him where he wouldn't have any questions. And he responded, "Yeah, that will never happen." And it never did.

Because he asked these questions, he was able to convey to others in the organization what it meant to be a business person. And because you had to interact with him, you knew he was going to ask these questions, and you realized you had to understand what you were doing and why, or he was going to expose the weaknesses in your plan. Once he felt I had mastered the art of business planning, the next exercise he challenged me on was to summarize the plan in a simple chart. I have thought about his examples for more than thirty years.

Similarly, Christ asked questions and was focused on empowering his disciples to take the narrow path and lead in a narrow way. He would chastise them, he would be critical of them, and then he would bring them up. It is that sense of creating a sense of urgency, challenging them, and then thanking them, building them back up, and empowering them for their future roles.

My mentor was a master of simplifying things. In looking at my plans, he would say, "There is probably a two-by-two chart we could create to simplify the plan." All the analysis simplified in a two by two, or a chart, or a one-page summary. Brilliant!

All of this helped me think critically so that when an issue arose, I almost immediately started to do a 360 analysis in my mind. How does this issue impact our board, our community, our doctors, our residents, our nurses, our service workers? How does it relate to our finances? How does it relate to our mission and to our strategies? How would an academic evaluate the situation? How would someone in supply chain look at the issue? You have to take a broad-based perspective, not just through a singular lens or focus. You can train yourself to do this; it's not rocket science. Some of this comes with experience, but some of it comes with the discipline to train your mind to have these critical business skills.

To create change, as you empower people, you motivate people by creating urgency either through operations, improvements, strategy, expense reductions, or all of the above. Christ led the most significant change in history.

Throughout my career, executives and their teams presented plans that were basically a list of the reasons they couldn't grow—we don't have money, we don't have resources, and so on. My usual response is, "Well, if I were a board member, if this is your vision and strategy, I would say sell your division." Of course, this makes the executives and teams understandably upset. But often, what happens next is that these teams begin to start to list all the things they could do, and they stop limiting themselves. They are charged up to put together a much more aggressive plan of action. And the result is that what ultimately is presented to the board is much more progressive.

These are not atypical moments. As a leader, some of this may be influenced by Christ's leadership example and how he managed situations, and some of it may just be stubbornness. When challenged, it is game on, and the team rises to the occasion. So as a result, instead of focusing on the status quo, the division is focusing on national programs and national partnerships that will extend our ability to enhance health and wellness.

Over the years, I have been a huge fan of "blue sky" sessions, where you are allowed to dream about what you could do if resources were no object. What is amazing is how many people totally dislike these sessions. Their concerns are that people will get the wrong idea or that it is not disciplined. But in every session I have ever attended, when people are allowed to dream even a little, novel and innovative ideas that otherwise would not have been considered are always identified.

Sometimes you have to pull out of people what they want to do, because for some reason they don't naturally do it. I tell people all the time, "You are not doing your job if we don't say no." You need to advocate and come at us with proposals that force us to say no. I know that oftentimes these asks are killed before they ever got to senior leadership. But you need to ask. For whatever reason, I don't understand why people don't do that all the time. It is about creating urgency to have a vision and take what you have to a higher level.

In one particular strategic planning meeting, we talked about how our organization is currently a $7 billion company, and in the next five years, we wanted to double our size to be a $15 billion corporation with a hundred thousand employees and the national brand. That might sound a little far-fetched, but when you looked at the history of the organization, we had doubled in size approximately every five years. So it was not an inconceivable idea. But even though that had been our long track record, many people could not believe that was truly possible.

That is what Christ did. He created urgency in the church and drove people to change.

6. Generating Short-Term Wins

Christ was focused on having a series of short-term wins that would all lead to the most significant, broad-based win ever—his death and resurrection. As metaphors for action, the miracles can easily be translated into examples of the kinds of short-term wins that Kotter references. His first of thirty-seven miracles was to turn water into wine at a wedding, which led to healing people, feeding thousands of people, catching fish to help feed thousands, and ultimately raising Lazarus from the dead. Each win generated additional wins that ultimately helped Christ achieve the mission. And the stakes for these wins got higher and higher toward the end of his life.

While he was building these immediate and powerful wins, there were occasions where Christ would perform a miracle and then tell the person impacted to not tell anyone. He would heal someone and say, "Don't tell anyone." He would say, "It is not my time to bring this all to the head." He was building a platform to carry on after his resurrection. Timing is everything in leadership, as it is in life!

The social determinants program we have been discussing was built on short-term wins. We would sometimes say to each other that it was better to be lucky than good, because with some of these ventures, we really didn't know that what we were doing would prove to lower health care costs. We did it because we believed what we were doing was right. We were hesitant to talk about the program initially but became more vocal as its successes became clear. And along the way, we were able to provide proof that addressing social determinants works. The focus first was on patients. But now we are also seeing impactful success with employers and employees. It all builds on itself to bigger and increasingly significant programs, like some of the work being done with personal determinants of health and structural and systemic racism. We kept asking, "What's next? Where is the need?"

7. Consolidating Gains and Producing More Change

Christ consolidated gains and then sought to produce even more and greater change. Christ's gains often were in his disciples and his apostles. He prepared his disciples to be ready when he left in making a lifelong change. In an American, falsely Christian way, some might suggest that Christ lost because he was crucified. But where he succeeded was through his resurrection and his people who continue to spread the Gospel even to this day.

Through the social determinants of health program, the greatest gains we achieved were in how we impacted people's lives. We aggregated those gains and began extending the program to employers and employees. We are extending the program to the personal determinants of health and now began talking about a health-risk appraisal that consolidates success from these efforts. We continued to expand how to address the racial determinants of health and are talking to other companies about looking at the social, personal, and racial determinants that impact health and well-being.

There are many examples in the Gospels where Christ consolidated gains leading to greater growth. In Acts, the personal problems the disciples exhibited previously seemed to go away, and they committed to servant leadership and having a transformational impact (Acts 17:6). The story of the church was about growth and achievement. The number of people baptized a day grew substantially (from three thousand to five thousand a day); the number of people turning to Christ grew, and the number of churches grew. There were stories about the victories over evil, healing diseases, and beating down poverty (Acts 4:32–37).

They were able to take these short-term successes, consolidate them, and continue to build the momentum that carried on throughout history. They were successful in taking their message and building on this foundation of Christian principles and the teaching and leadership of Christ.

What we found was that how we could extend the reach of the social determinants program was nearly endless. For example, our organization and the <u>Green and Healthy Homes Initiative</u> (GHHI) recently announced the launch of a partnership to improve the health of individuals and communities by improving the safety and energy efficiency of homes in several major cities. Housing is critical, an area where my organization didn't doesn't have expertise. We couldn't solve for every social determinant, but we could with partners that had expertise in certain areas. Green and Healthy Homes Initiative knows about housing and interventions to improve housing security for all. At some point, we should consider turning the American health system into a public health system as well and change the investment model.

8. Anchoring New Approaches in the Culture

Christ was able to accomplish this in a number of ways. He was able to get out the word through his disciples and apostles. The four Gospels were written along with the New Testament to memorialize Christ's actions. Through his ministry, there was a succession of gains that ultimately created this revolutionary impact that changed the world.

Anchoring changes like the social determinants into the culture of the organization, you want to get the momentum going forward with such intensity and volume that it becomes embedded in everything you do as an organization and you can never turn back. That is by communication, by leadership, by resourcing it, by proving that you have had success, and by making sure it is on a path that you wouldn't want to undo.

Thinking about retirement in the years ahead, there is a natural concern that what has been accomplished will erode over time or even be thrown out the door. And while you can never guarantee what will happen as you leave an organization, there are steps that can be taken to help ensure that a leader's vision for an organization moves forward after he or she is gone. For that, it is helpful to think about and look at Christ's example of how he developed his disciples and created an ultimate succession plan—in our next chapter.

TEN

LEADERSHIP DEVELOPMENT: FISHERS OF MEN

Over the years, I have often had the opportunity to teach classes in leadership and leadership development. I keep a file of articles that impact me, and as time rolled along, these articles became an evolving outline to help guide my talks about what leadership might look like. What developed was a guide with ten major principles that I think about regarding leadership:

1. *Create your story.* Most people, it seems, tend to live chaotic lives and don't seem to have real purpose. Spend some time thinking about what you want your legacy to be. You want to think about how to use whatever influence you have in purposeful and thoughtful ways. As a Christian, what is your life purpose and life signature?

2. *Constantly focus on priorities.* First, you want to keep your life purpose front and center. The decisions you make should be based on that. Try to connect with interesting people. Have a plan and live in the now. This area is incredibly important in balancing faith, family, career, hobbies, fitness, and other interests.

3. *Remember the importance of humility.* This relates to servant leadership, the Beatitudes, and having social responsibility. You have to develop a mindset to be thankful and live with a sense of gratitude. You want to own your mistakes. And it is important to focus on volunteerism.

4. *Ninety percent of failures relate to interpersonal competencies.* This is all about emotional intelligence, which Christ had in abundance.[1]

Leadership is all about relationships. Talent alone is not enough. You want to be constantly connecting the dots. Establish communities and focus on others. Bring people along. And develop habits of optimism. You only have to look to Christ as the perfect example of emotional intelligence.

5. *Focus consistently on how you create culture.* Very successful people understand what motivates people and can create meaning for people that connects to the organizational mission. Having the ability to help people understand and deal with change is critical as you create culture. Praise publicly but criticize privately.

6. *Push to do better.* As I have said previously, one of the keys to leading change is to create a sense of urgency. That is all about pushing people to do better.

7. *Learn to listen! Look! Ask questions!* It is a little about visual literacy where you need to learn to listen, learn to see, and then learn to ask questions. The idea is to sit back and listen, gather information, explore alternatives, analyze, discuss, act, and evaluate. Practice intellectual empathy. Know people where they came from. You want to understand people and what might have happened in their lives. Once you know their story, it can tell you a lot.

8. *Avoid the fatal mistake.* Live a life of integrity. Character counts. Character determines your destiny. We all make mistakes, and the key is to turn to Christ when you mess up.

9. *At the end of life, people talk about family and faith.* It is not how much money you made. It is not your work. It is not your diplomas that measure your worth. It's really your family and faith. Most people talk about family at the end of life. A smaller subset will also talk about faith.

10. *You are (and always will be) an incomplete leader.* This is kind of an overarching theme in life, that you will always be an incomplete leader. It ties back directly to the concept of servant leadership.

I have continued to refine and rework these principles over the years, and I probably always will as I keep learning. But this has been a solid foundation for me. And over the years, I have continued to expand on these principles and developed a philosophy and approach regarding leadership development that follows. Some years, I may emphasize a smaller set of these principles, and at other times, I have used them all. The point though is for a person to have their own goals, their own principles, and their own plan. From a Christian leadership perspective, it is necessary to think about the way you want your faith to influence your plan.

Tie Your Top Button

A first step in leadership development is having a solid base relative to your faith, with confidence in your ability and approach, and even having a philosophy of how you want to manage people and situations. Always think about the times you need to "tie your top button," stroll to the podium, and talk. You have things framed up regarding what you are going to say and how you are going to say it. Having that foundation, in addition to having a well-rounded education, will help in the long term as a Christian leader.

Look Inside First

An initial step in leadership development is to look inside first, because that is where it all starts. In Mark 7:20–23, Christ talks about how what comes out of a person's heart is what defines and defiles them. That relates to what you put into your body spiritually as well as physically, abiding in Christ, who you hang with, what you focus on every day. We all make mistakes. We all have lapses. But then you come back to and abide in Christ. You make sure from the inside out you are thinking and living the Christian life, not getting caught up in the world. And then you get really focused on your conviction to be a leader in Christ's image. That conviction includes not just your beliefs but also the values you use, the commitments you make, and the motivation you have in dealing with the challenges of each day.

Personal Journey or Organizational Responsibility

I think there is a little bit of both personal and organizational responsibility in leadership development. You own your own development. And 80–90 percent of your success depends on how you manage your boss. The same thing with the personal journey. The organization has a responsibility to help employees with their personal development and make opportunities to see a path and where they can go in the organization. But there is a significant part of your leadership development you have to know yourself and take responsibility for. The organization is not going to do it. You have to keep developing, keep evolving, keep learning. You owe it to yourself. You can't wait for the organization to tell you what to do.

Knowing Who You Are and Where You Are Going

To be successful at leadership development, you have to have a solid understanding of where you stand relative to leadership as well as the culture of your organization. The other day, I was looking at LinkedIn and noticed one of our employees who had posted a comment and talked about our organization being a place of servant leadership. Those words are increasingly finding a place in our narrative, not by any mandate I or others have made but because it is becoming more of the organic culture of the organization.

At a recent video program for our leadership group, Vic Strecher and I were talking about life purpose, and he asked me about my life purpose. I answered that my faith is what motivates me and provides my life purpose. In previous years, I might not have been as comfortable talking about that because technically I do not work for a faith-based organization. On the other hand, we are a place that accepts and provides care for all faiths. After that program, I had a number of people text me and email me who said, "Thank you for sharing that. I always knew that to be true, but I am glad you said it out loud."

I have been given opportunities and resources, and in the end, I will be judged on how I use those resources. I am much more comfortable with those words being part of the organization.

A Similar Approach to Leadership

I know that a number of people in our organization who are in leadership positions are people of strong faith. There has been no official mandate to hire people of faith, but it happens over time. I never ask, and the company does not ask. These people are solid leaders in their own right, with a similar mindset to mine regarding leadership. And they happen to be people of faith. They are Catholic, Missouri Lutheran, German Protestant, and other religious denominations. Some are agnostic. But we all have a similar mindset, similar values, and a similar approach to leadership.

Mission and Leadership Development

It is important, particularly for younger employees, to understand the mission of the organization and have a purpose at work. You create purpose at work through the mission and values. This is what we were always trying to do, this is what we were about, and this was how we do it. It is part aspirational, part inspirational, and part practical. And it is increasingly clear that organizations must align their missions with those of the individual employee. We worked hard over the last several years to help our people think differently about what they were doing and why. And I think we were successful. We were in a transitional phase from a regional to a national organization. We were in the process of changing our mission, which you never do lightly. We were transitioning from a hospital-based organization to an organization focused on health and well-being. We began investing in things we never invested in before. As we were doing that, we are always thinking about how we could people along and communicate to them. Helping other leaders understand that vision and being able to articulate it and motivate employees to aspire to that vision is job one as a leader.

You have to think about how to constantly push the organization to the next level. How do you talk to employees about where we are at as an organization, and where we are going, and what we are going to do after that? Christ took people who were uneducated and not leaders, and then as he got closer to death, he pushed harder, encouraging his people to push harder, helping them understand that they needed to lead. And that is true for leaders overall. One of the key aspects for any leader is to think about what's next. Where do we go now that we are here?

The Importance of Mentors

Very early in my career, I had a mentor when I was working in Minneapolis who pulled me aside before I went into an important meeting. He said, "Here's the deal. Walk into this meeting. Pull yourself up to the table and sit up straight. Put your forearms on the table, not your elbows, make pleasant small talk before the meeting, and keep your mouth shut during the meeting. You have to make eye contact. I'll tell you later when you can talk." I was scared to death and didn't say a word.

After the meeting, he took me aside and asked me what I thought of the meeting. After that meeting and others, he would discuss why people said what they said, interactions and reactions of the group to what was said, their nonverbals, and other group dynamics. After several meetings, he leaned over to me before the meeting and whispered, "You can talk now." The point was to sit back and listen, get a lay of the land, be careful what you say, and know your audience. So many people are so quick to talk. They are thinking about how they want to impress others and what they are going to say and not listening to what anyone else is saying.

Another person I worked for I watched carefully. He used a red pen. And while people were presenting, he would write questions in a corner of the document. After the presentation, he would let everyone else talk. And as people asked the questions he had written, he would cross them off. At the end, he would ask questions that no one else thought to ask. To this day, I often do that same thing. The people I have really admired in my career are the people who ask the right questions.

Many of us have also worked for leaders where we learned what not to do. Some people I worked for were very strategic people, but I completely disagreed with how they wanted to execute the strategy. People who are ultra-aggressive would say to threaten a potential partner if they didn't work with us. Some people were only driven by ego, entitlement, and hierarchy and were generally mean-spirited.

I have never had a pastor who I could say was a mentor in my life. In fact, over time, this has been an area that was increasingly a disconnect in my faith and view of leadership. I had a pastor once who told me I needed to quit my job and change careers so I could spend more time in the church. And realistically, I couldn't do that. Still, the pastor was very aggressive and questioned my priorities. That was not useful. My wife and I have also attended very insular churches that were in such contrast to my job that they were of little support in my day-to-day life. To be honest, churches are often disappointing to many people. If you know that, you can manage your expectations.

I have had two church pastors where I found myself taking notes, because I could use what they said in my daily leadership thinking and work. It was information I could use in my day-to-day life. They are all really good at weaving stories together. But typically, pastors have not been useful in my work, which is really kind of sad. Pastors may think they are leaders, and they do operationally lead churches, but they can lack the dynamics of a real leader. I had one pastor tell me it is more important to have an MBA than to study theology, particularly in terms of running the business of the church, and that numbers (how big, how many) were the most important measure of success. Some church organizations think that as the church leader becomes a better business leader, everyone wins. And maybe we will sprinkle in a little religion here and there, but keep focused on the numbers. From a faith standpoint, that is a dangerous message, because once it is all about the numbers, you are not doing God's work. When we do this, we do an injustice to Christ and his great leadership by not looking to him as an example for leadership; instead, we are looking at the big business leader of the day or the big megachurch pastor for inspiration.

Assembling Your Team

When you think about starting a ministry (or leading an organization), if you pick the wealthy, the rich, the powerful, the politicians, the artists, the athletes, and the stars of the day, it would send one message to the masses, probably one they would view with skepticism. Christ picked the most common of the common. It required, particularly initially, a lot more time, because they were rough around the edges. After spending time with too many politicians, I see why Christ stayed away from them.

Jesus selected twelve men who were poorly educated from less than stellar backgrounds. They were at times cowards and doubters and not always cooperative. But the leadership of Christ and these twelve men led to the most significant change the world has ever known. The call to faith in our Lord, Jesus Christ!

When you think about the disciples, they were fishermen, tax collectors, and the like. He only picked twelve. Selecting the number twelve had some historic significance. He probably thought about how many people he could actually manage, just like leaders think about today. Instead of fishermen, they became fishers of men under Christ's guidance. Christ created a vision. Some dropped their nets and followed immediately; others needed a bit more persuasion. And that is the first step of leadership: to pick your own team.

The Disciples: Woefully Unprepared

As described in previous chapters, the twelve disciples Jesus picked had many failings. They were unprepared, they lacked perspective and vision themselves, they often drew wrong conclusions, and they even rejected Christ. There were times when they clearly just didn't get the parables (Mark 4:13). They had their own desires and reasons for following Christ. They were overconfident and had petty squabbles over rank and who was the greatest among them. At other times, they lacked confidence. When there was the storm at sea, even though Peter, Andrew, James, and John were experienced fishermen, they were afraid of being shipwrecked. Jesus calmed the waters and had to build their confidence, telling them to "have faith" (Mark 4:40).

At times, they were great examples of people who didn't understand the message of servant leadership. They would get angry at people who wanted to bring children in need to Christ—even though he was a champion for children. The disciples made strong statements that they would die for Jesus, but they betrayed him at critical junctures. They drew wrong conclusions from things he told them. They failed, and yet Christ kept working with them, developing them, making them ready for their time to carry the message. And despite their failings, the disciples became faithful witnesses to Christ.

Maybe we shouldn't be so hard on the disciples, however. The parables challenge all of us as we read them. And overconfidence, a lack of confidence, drawing wrong conclusions, not understanding, being unprepared, and lacking perspective are weaknesses we all experience during our lives.

Bringing Your Team Along

Jesus adapted his leadership to the realities of the situation. He instructed the disciples when they were uninformed, directed them when they were confused, prodded them when they were reluctant, and encouraged them when they were downhearted. When they were ready, he allowed them limited task and responsibilities and then participated with them, guiding them through their assignments. Finally, he empowered them and commissioned them as his apostles.

Christ never gave up on his team. He brought them along and mentored them. He gave them the values, the Great Commission, and the Beatitudes to serve as principles to guide them. And he slowly empowered them and gave them more authority. He sent them out into the world, giving them instructions, telling them to take nothing for the journey, no staff, no bag, no bread, no shirt. If someone questioned what you were doing, you had to leave town (Luke 9:1–6).

He sent a real message that they needed to trust in Him and in God and that they would provide, with the power of the Holy Spirit, to inspire and support them (Mark 6:7). It is similar to any leader: you keep your people close, you nurture them, you teach them, and then you send them out. And when Christ sent his disciples out, he often sent them out in groups, not often alone, for support, which are the things you might do today with young leaders.

The Cost of Being a Disciple—Discipline, Hard Work

The foundation you are given as a Christian leader is often invisible, but it provides strength and stability in making decisions. There are no shortcuts, no easy buttons to push in building that solid foundation for life.

Molding your heart and your outlook to achieve the values of the Beatitudes is challenging. When you look at the examples of Christ, you see how he related to people and embodied the love of people, but when it came to taking on forces of authority, he wasn't bashful at all.

Servant leadership is in complete contrast to authoritarian leadership and the concept that leaders are born with a certain DNA and a certain quality. Becoming a servant leader requires time and action. The action is framed in your heart and mind and expressed through the opportunities and resources you are given in life. If you have these opportunities and resources, and you don't apply those gifts to helping others, then you have missed the mark.

John and James, for example, were not men of immediate form; they were hearty souls who had lived a rough life. As they first heard the Beatitudes and Great Commission, these words and accompanying actions would be in stark contrast to what they had experienced in their lives as Christ recruited them to his cause.

It seems inconsistent to select these people to be the disciples that would create a worldwide movement. And then you look at Christ's ability to change them and create this movement. It is powerful.

Comforting and Supporting the Team

While Christ could be hard on his disciples as he developed them, he also spent time comforting them and reassuring them. In John 14:1, he says, "Do not let your hearts be troubled ..." As a leader, you create a sense of urgency and you challenge people, but there is a fine line between challenging people as well as acknowledging them and telling them they are doing a great job, to keep it up.

He provided help as he challenged them. For example, in John 14:26, he says, "But the Advocate, the Holy Spirit, whom the Father will send in my name, will teach you all things and will remind you of everything I have said to you." He provided practical advice; he showed the example of prayer, the example of compassion to all people, how to relate to people who weren't in authority; and he gave them tools and the power of the Holy Spirit, which would provide guidance and comfort throughout their lives.

One of my leadership regrets is not praying and listening more to the Holy Spirit. This may sound a little weird, but stay with me for a minute. As the scripture passage above notes, it is the Holy Spirit who teaches us, reminds us, and guides us. The challenge for each of us is to pray and listen. We will talk more about this in the chapter on gaining perspective.

Abide by the Beatitudes

The Gospels, and particularly in John, spend time talking about abiding (the word is mentioned sixty times in the Gospel according to John), which means to endure, to remain, to stay on, to hold on, to endure. And that is a quality that leaders and Christian leaders should maintain. Staying true to your foundation helps ground you—your heart, mind, and soul. Applying the principles of the Beatitudes—such as meekness, humility, and treating people with respect—is extremely important, and you want to stay rooted in these values. When you see people who acquire money and power, often they change and no longer abide by these values.

How do you keep from being corrupted by the trappings of being a leader? People give you attention, and they tell you that what you are doing is great, even when it is not. To say it directly, they tell you how great you are. People start to think about what they deserve. And so it is hard to stay grounded. If you're not grounded and don't abide in Jesus and God, you are likely to abide in something else. It is definitely a trap in life of which you need to be constantly aware.

Throughout my career, as people in executive positions would move on, people would often lobby to take those positions, often taking the posture that they deserved this promotion, with all the attendant drama and politics.

As a leader, a great idea is to have the Beatitudes on a card on your desk, where you see them every day as a reminder to abide by these values.

A Christian Leader's Job Description

Any human resources department can send you the competencies they use for their leadership and executive leadership teams. And as you review these, you should think about what competencies might be included in a job description for a Christian leader. After a bit of noodling, I came up with this:

Christian Leader's Job Description

Title	Christian leader
Supervisor	Jesus Christ
Job Summary, Main Responsibilities, and Accountabilities	• The Christian leader works in all types of settings, roles, and responsibilities. • They bring to their position a commitment to serve Jesus Christ over anything else. • They are committed daily to serving God, utilizing the skills listed below. • They are responsible for making a spiritual impact on their environment and the people they work with. • They will be accountable for the impact they made relative to the resources and opportunities they have had in life. • They strive to live a life modeled in scripture and powered by the Holy Spirit, journeying down the narrow path of Christian life, serving God and seeking his purpose, and knowing one's only hope is Jesus Christ.

Key Competencies	• *Follows and lives the Great Commandment.* Loves God with mind, body, soul. Loves their neighbor.
	• *Follows and lives the Great Commission.* Shares the good news and makes disciples of all nations.
	• *Applies the ideals of the Beatitudes every day.*
	   o poor in spirit (Matthew 5:3)
	   o ability to mourn (Matthew 5:4)
	   o meek (Matthew 5:5)
	   o hunger and thirst for righteousness (Matthew 5:6)
	   o merciful (Matthew 5:7)
	   o pure in heart (Matthew 5:8)
	   o peacemaker (Matthew 5:9)

Other Key Attributes	• Ability to withstand persecution, insults, and false kinds of evils (Matthew 5:10–12) • Prays without ceasing, ability to make disciples abide in God's Word (John 8:31–32) • Is nonjudgmental • Exhibits the imagination and innovation of a child • Exhibits courage • Meets people where they are at • Is self-aware and focuses on their own behavior first, not the behavior of others

	• Asks questions and listens first • Is a good steward • Has a clear understanding that it is not what we say but what we do with our blessing that is most important
Education and Work Experience	• No advance degree required; biblical knowledge required; embodied by the Holy Spirit, marked by confidence in God (Matthew 19:26)
Location	• Anywhere in the world
Remuneration	• Eternal life

When I looked at our organization's leadership and executive competencies recommendations, many competencies listed could be applied to the leadership example of Christ. The competencies included builds effective teams, communicates effectively, drives engagement, instills trust, manages conflict, drives results, strategic mindset, creates shared vision and culture, and motivates and develops others. These are all competencies that Jesus had to the max.

Character Traits of Leaders

Courage

Courage isn't about taking unnecessary risks. It comes from a belief that what you are doing is more important than the fear of not doing it. With your faith, what does courage mean? Is it courage to live your faith? Courage to share your faith, particularly in a secular work setting? There are ways to share your faith without being overtly Christian. You can refer to your pastor, your church.

Some would say you need to use your faith as a blunt instrument. And there may be a time and place to do that. But I think for most of us, it is having the courage to artfully know who you are and what you believe.

As part of an experiment, researchers put up a big bulletin board in a park in Lower Manhattan, Lieutenant Petrosino Square.[2] At the top of the bulletin board, written in chalk, was the question "What is your biggest regret?" At first people walked by, but then people began to write on the bulletin board and talk. As the board filled up with regrets, the research found something interesting. No one regretted the things they did. They regretted the things they didn't do; chances not taken; words not spoken; dreams never pursued. People needed to have the courage to step out and act—and do something. You are going to be in the arena, and you're going to be bloody, but at least you are in the arena, in the fight, as opposed to being in the stands with people throwing rocks at you. The point is, if you are working to try to take a stand and make the world better, you are going to get criticized for that.

I regret that I didn't correct my thinking about leadership to mirror the leadership example of Christ sooner. I regret not praying and listening to the Holy Spirit every hour of my life. I regret that I looked to secular leaders, not Jesus Christ, for examples of leadership. I regret that I didn't keep the Beatitudes more front and center in my life. I regret that I wasn't a better son, brother, husband, father, friend, leader, and follower.

That is what Christ told his disciples. "Go, don't take anything with you, and have courage. I have prepared you, and I am always here to help you."

Christ exhibited tremendous courage throughout as he took on the establishment of the day. He cleared the temple of merchants and money changers as they were disrupting worship. He exhorted them to "Stop turning my Father's house into a market!" (John 2:16). At times, he didn't keep Sabbath the way some regional leaders wanted, which took courage during that day. And nothing could illustrate courage more than the events leading up to his crucifixion. The temple leaders questioned his authority; the Pharisees and other religious leaders questioned him about the greatest commandment; he was beaten and then crucified. He knew what was coming, what he had to go through, yet he had the courage to go through all that.

One minute he was holding children, and the next he was creating a riot at the temple. There is an interesting dynamic in terms of emotion and how he lived his life.

As I have gotten older, I think I have gotten more courage. It is all about being more confident in who you are and what you believe, and even in your own skill set, whatever that might be. It is about the ability to have courage about voicing your opinion to give people critical feedback. For example, if you have empathy for someone, it may require you to have courage to give them some critical feedback in order to help them grow. I always tell my wife that I am now doing things and saying things that when I was younger

I would not have done because I was not confident enough. You have to have the confidence to have the courage to speak and act, whether that is with your boss, board members, or anyone in a position of authority. I regret not speaking up more.

When you think of your obligation, you want to make sure you are empathetic and willing to argue for people, to relate to them, and to put yourself in their place.

It goes back to a philosophy of leadership. You start to frame up for yourself how you view being a leader, and once you get that set, it's about having the courage to do it. Then you have an ability to be more forceful.

Don't Judge

We live in a society where people are very quick to judge and condemn. But it is not ours to judge. In Matthew 7:1–2, Jesus says, "Do not judge, or you too will be judged. For in the same way you judge others, you will be judged, and with the measure you use, it will be measured to you." Don't presume you know what is in someone's head. What you need to do is try to understand the other person's story. It is how you treat people and give them the benefit of the doubt until you understand their story.

It is interesting that as organizations grow and acquire new companies, the cultures of the partnering organizations can be so different from each other. One company may bring great expertise, and that will help the combined organizations grow in many ways, but many times leaders can be very judgmental, defensive, and unable to get out of their own way in how they view leadership and culture. It takes years to change that type of culture. Some are smart enough to pick up the rhetoric of the incomplete leader when I talk about it, but by their actions, I don't think they really believe it yet.

Compassion

Another critical characteristic of a Christian leader is compassion. Christ was compassionate to those who really needed it. He didn't judge the woman at the well even though she had been married five times and was living in sin with another man. He said to her, "Woman, go and sin no more." We could all judge a lot less and show compassion a lot more. We need to focus on being merciful by forgiving the fallen, helping the hurting, finding patience with difficult people, showing kindness to enemies, and caring for those who are lost.

When you think about what success is for a Christian leader, it can be challenging in the business world. Business is about profits, revenue growth, and making great products and services. For the individual, it may be about making a lot of money. How does this square, then, with being a servant leader and modeling Christ's leadership example? Is success then about fighting for equality and having compassion for others? Is it about using your resources to help others?

Christian leadership is indeed about being a compassionate servant leader. But the truth and irony for Christians is that it is about both compassion and making profits and great products. Clayton Christensen was a very well-known academic and influential business consultant and Harvard professor, and in a 2010 *Harvard Business Review* article, he asked the question, "How will you measure your life?"[3] It is a great question and a great way to think about how you will measure the success of your overall leadership style and how you impact your work life and connect it to your daily life and your pursuit of faith.

Leaders Walk toward Trouble

In John 11:1–10, Jesus tells the disciples that they are returning to Judea, a place the disciples remind Jesus is where there were those who tried to stone him. And yet Jesus wants to return to that environment. That is what true leaders do; they are willing to walk where others might not go, which is part of the hard work of being a disciple. You don't want to walk away from trouble; walk in. That is what Christ did.

Extend Grace

The first thing Christ said to the disciples at the moment he was reunited with the disciples following the resurrection was "Peace be with you." He extended his grace. He always extended grace. Think about the moments in your life when someone extended grace to you, and those times when you have had opportunities to extend grace. You can do this when you frame up your mind and your attitude so that in tough situations, you can be in the right position mentally to react with grace. We are incomplete, and Christ calls on us all to extend grace to everyone.

In the same way that we extend grace to others, it is a gift for us as well, because doing so provides internal peace, confidence, and assurance to us through the Holy Spirit as we go about our daily lives.

Carry Your Corner

In the book *The Purpose Gap*, the author Patrick Reyes recounts a story about the Rev. Dr. Otis Moss III's analysis of Jesus helping a paralytic man in Luke 5:17–26.[4] In that story, four men use a mat to carry the man to Jesus, each taking a corner of the mat, and by each carrying their corners, they are able to get the man to Jesus to be healed. That is what we as leaders must do. We pick up the corners for one another and continue to reinforce that concept for one another.

Imagination and Innovation: To Think like a Child

In Matthew 18:3, Jesus teaches his followers, "Unless you change and become like little children, you will never enter the kingdom of heaven." This is another indicator of how Christ supported and accepted children, but it is also a key to many other things like acceptance, innocence, and innovation. To think like a child and take that leap of imagination needed, either to be born again or in finding new ways of doing things, is a critical characteristic of a leader. You have to have an open mind and continue to learn. To have that open mind is critical to having an innovative culture. Being more like a child, with an inquisitive mind, looking at new and fresh ways to do things, is the essence of Christian leadership. Do you have a growth mindset or a fixed mindset related to how we learn, our attitude, our culture, and our ability?[5] Christ was all about a growth mindset and that idea of the power to do things to help others.

You start to think about your role in life. You will accomplish less with a limited view. Better to take a broader view and work toward it.

Stewardship

Another key characteristic of leadership is the need to be a good steward. And the Gospels have several stories related to that, including the parable of the bags of gold and the parable of the shrewd manager, to name just two (Matthew 25:14–30, Luke 16:1–9). This is all about being judged for what you have been given in life and what you do with the resources you have available.

As Jim Collins said in his book *Good to Great and the Social Sectors*, we all need to make an impact relative to our resources. When you think about this from a Christian perspective, you are going to be judged by the impact you made in life relative to those resources. You were blessed, you were given these opportunities, you were given these resources, not only in comparison to your neighborhood and the city you live in but the world. As Americans, we are the richest country in the world, but what have we done with our resources to make the impact we should have? As churches, what impact are we making on lives, including those you worship with and those you do not?

Succession Planning

When you talk to people who have retired about planning for retirement, they almost all say it is critical to find the right balance. When thinking about the organization you work for, it comes down to trying to ensure and finding the right mix of leadership skills in the organization to help ensure that the current culture of the organization and focus of the organization continues.

Succession planning involves not only putting personnel in place to continue the mission and vision but also about putting the infrastructure in place to help continue the momentum. Jesus was thoughtful about what was to come after his death, his succession plan. He talked about the church to come after he was gone. He told Peter that he was the rock on which he would build his church. He suggested ways his disciples could bring disputes to the church for resolution.

He planned to spread the word to people as he was prepared for the crucifixion. He was relying on the people who he identified and basically said, "You are the people who will carry on my message." And in the case of Christ, there was the guiding Spirit for the disciples.

If you believe in the Trinity, God created the earth, he came as a man through Christ to save us, and part of it is an ongoing basis, as he is there as the Holy Spirit, leading us and guiding us every day.

I have been in and witnessed multiple succession processes. Some went very well, and others did not. The boards and CEO think about who is in what role and how to have the right people in the mix. And, of course, as you do that, sometimes people who feel they should be in certain positions can become upset, and you have to deal with that. We set up a process with various personalities and skill sets that will help the organization continue to grow in the future.

For me, it has always been about putting things in place to hopefully ensure that the organization will continue to expand the programs I care about—such as continuing to address health equity and the social determinants of health. We want to continue to move beyond what is considered traditional and impact people's lives where they live, helping ensure there is a safe home, an educational pipeline, financial security, and food security, among other basic needs. We want to continue to help people with the resources they need to make lives better. We want to ensure that the economic development programs, neighborhood programs, and an established grocery store in a neighborhood that was previously a food desert all involve concrete pieces of infrastructure that hopefully will be maintained. But there are no promises; you can only do your best to put things in place to continue to move programs forward.

ELEVEN

CULTIVATE AND COMMUNICATE: SPREAD THE GOOD NEWS

Included in the Great Commission (Matthew 28:18–20) is the idea that as you go and make disciples of nations, you will share the good news. And isn't that what we do as Christian leaders? We communicate and cultivate relationships. That is true of great leaders, whether or not you are motivating them to be Christians or motivating them to do anything in life.

Words matter. Christ understood this all too well.

I grew up in a community where the churches were very focused on doctrine, with lots of debate about the fine points of scripture. My background shaped my view of biblical Christianity, but it also made for difficult times as we moved and experienced many who had a limited appreciation of doctrine, and we found it increasingly hard to apply in our daily lives. Christ made his narrative available for the least of these, the people he called. He was able to communicate in a very strong way, in a way people would relate to and understand. He used examples from the day. No one was better at it.

There was no printing press. No internet. He had to rely on his ability as an oral communicator. Christ took it down to the basics of basics in ways people would relate to.

In his communication and in the narrative created in the Gospels, Christ exemplifies some great communication techniques that are the foundation for strong leadership communication today.

Although he never stated it, Christ understood the communication process in changing behaviors. First you create awareness, then you change perceptions, which ultimately leads to advocacy, which then leads to changing behaviors and creating change. When you think about how our organization has addressed the social determinants of health and health equity, we had to work for years to increase awareness about how the societal factors influence health and well-being, to set the stage for what needed to be done (to be honest, we are still working at establishing the need not only locally but nationally), to get the ball rolling, and then we began to see advocacy taking place and behavior change and action to truly address these issues.

A lot of it goes down to being passionate in what you believe in. What are you trying to do? What are you trying to accomplish? And then how you communicate and build relationships.

A Master of Words

I am not sure where I heard it, but I remember being struck by a panelist at a conference I was attending commenting that data often doesn't matter, but words and stories do. The example he used was that of health inequities. Data has shown for decades that the color of skin has a significant impact on the health care services you will get. Testing, procedures, surgeries, and so forth all can be different if you happen to not be white. We could discuss inequities more, but the point is that the inequities of care were known but largely ignored. The power of the stories of people like Serena Williams and those impacted by COVID created a national focus.

Serena's story starts with a health scare after the birth of her daughter in September 2017. A world-class athlete, winner of twenty-three Grand Slam titles in tennis, and with a number one ranking for over three hundred weeks, Serena had to beg her caregivers to believe her that something was wrong.

It turns out she had a pulmonary embolism, where one or more of the lungs are blocked by a blood clot, causing incredible pain and shortness of breath. She noted after she recovered that she thought she was going to die.

Sadly, it took her story and others to create the attention that these inequities require.

While the recorded history of His words and stories were captured for only a brief time during His ministry, Christ's words spoke volumes.

The first words recorded of Jesus speaking is when he was twelve years old, which I talked about in the chapter on purpose. Early on, His words clearly define who He was and was going to be.

The Passover was a major Jewish holiday that celebrated the Israelites being freed from slavery and leaving Egypt. Joseph, Mary, and Jesus made their pilgrimage to Jerusalem, and when they had been there the necessary days, they began their travels home. His parents assumed He was in the caravan returning to their home and were shocked and extremely concerned to find He was not with the caravan. Returning to Jerusalem to look for Him, they finally found Jesus in the temple after three days of searching. Jesus had stayed in Jerusalem in the temple courts, sitting among the teachers and asking them many questions (Luke: 2:46). It goes on to say that everyone who heard Him was amazed at what He said. Even as a young person, Jesus clearly showed His parents and others that He was different. His life was following a different path, a path dedicated to serving His Father.

When his parents saw Him, they were astonished. His mother said to him, "Son, why have you treated us like this? Your father and I have been anxiously searching for you." Luke 2:48–49 says, "Why were you looking for me?" he asked, "Did you not know that I had to be in my Father's House?"

His baptism is another example of some of His first recorded words. Jesus traveled to see John the Baptist at the Jordan River to be baptized. John was the appointed messenger of God to travel around and proclaim the coming of the Messiah to the people in Jerusalem and Judea. Clearly, John was pointing people to the path of Jesus Christ. As Jesus approached the Jordan River to be baptized, John declared to Jesus, as recorded in Matthew 3:13, "I need to be baptized by you." Jesus's response is interesting. As verse 15 goes on to say, "Let it be so now, for thus it is fitting for us to fulfill all righteousness." For many, Jesus's response is a bit unclear as to its meaning. For me, John's response showed he knew that this was the Messiah, and Jesus's response confirms that this was necessary to start Jesus's ministry and to start the call to a new way of life, a new path to follow. After His baptism, we are told in Matthew 3:16–17 that the "heaven was opened and he saw the spirit of God descending like a dove and alighting on him. And a voice said This is my Son, whom I love, with Him I am well pleased."

One of the more popular passages of scripture describes Jesus passing by the Sea of Galilee, seeing Simon and his brother Andrew casting their nets into the sea. Jesus said to them, "Come after me, and I will make you fishers of men." You can only imagine their thoughts. *Fishers of men? What is that all about?* Following Jesus was going down a new path that was focused on saving men's souls, a call for each of them to live a radically new life. Matthew 4:19 tells us that after hearing Christ's call, they left immediately, leaving everything behind, and stepped out onto the path of new life.

The words Jesus spoke at the beginning of His public ministry are recorded in Matthew 4:17, "Repent of your sins and turn to God, for the Kingdom of Heaven is near." In calling James, John, Andrew, and Peter from their lives as fishermen, his first charge to them was to repent of their sins and turn down a path—turn to God.

One of the significant parts of Jesus's public ministry is His temptation by the devil, soon after being baptized by John the Baptist. We are told that Jesus fasted forty days and nights in the Judean desert, where Satan attempted to get Jesus to sin. Among His words in Luke 4, the response to His temptation was the idea of man not living on bread alone, that we are to only worship the Lord our God and not to put God to the test. Jesus's response to temptation early in His ministry stands in contrast to the temptation of Adam and Eve. Jesus was walking down a different path.

Jesus's first sermon, the Sermon on the Mount, also stands in contrast to the actions of the religious and government leaders of the day. Matthew 5 offers a whole new narrative. Blessed are the poor in spirit, those who mourn, those who are meek, those who hunger and thirst for righteousness, the merciful, the pure in heart, the peacemakers, and those who are persecuted and insulted. These Beatitudes stand in sharp contrast to the religious and secular leaders of Jesus's time, and still today, they stand in sharp contrast to what we hear from our leaders, especially those in politics and in the secular world.

Earlier, I talked about the seven "I am" statements. They are profound examples of the impact of His words and form the basis of His ministry and who He was. These seven statements convey His love, the essence of His life, and that He is the way to a new life. They make clear to His followers who He was and what His values were, and they lay out why people should follow His leadership—a leadership built around the power of His words and His deeds. Jesus used words and stories to impact people's minds and hearts. His words give us a picture of His approach and style that went a radically different path from the religious leaders of the day.

Jesus's first word from the cross is found in Luke 23:34, which says, "Father, forgive them for they know not what they do." And they cast lots to divide His garments. Given the beatings, ridicule, and physical punishment that Jesus received, it's amazing to think that in His first words, He speaks of forgiveness. Clearly, Jesus's words demonstrate His love, a love born out of a different life, one of the narrow path.

After His resurrection, Jesus appears to His disciples. Luke 24:26 describes them recounting what has taken place on the road to Emmaus, where Jesus appeared to two men walking along and their describing to Him the events of the last days. While they were still speaking about this, He stood in the midst and said to them, "Peace be with you." But they were startled and terrified and thought they were seeing a ghost. Then He said to them, "Why are you troubled? And what questions arose in your hearts?" Depending on the translation you look at, the word *peace* can be found three to four hundred times in scripture. While it may seem a curious choice of word for Jesus's return from the tomb, it is quite consistent with His ministry. Peace can be used in different ways, but one would think that here, Christ is pointing to the absence of a life of chaos and noise found in the secular world, promoting the idea of finding peace through a right relationship with one another and our Lord Jesus Christ. As Isaiah 9:6 declares, "For to us a child is born, to us a son is given, and the government will be on His shoulder. And he will be called Wonderful Counselor, Might God, Everlasting Father, Prince of Peace Jesus sacrifice allowed man's relationship with to be peacefully restored." And as He states in John 14:27, "Peace I leave with you; my peace I give you. I do not give to you as the world gives. Do not let your hearts be troubled and do not be afraid."

Example after example, we see that Jesus's words were directed to changing hearts, minds, and souls. While we know words and stories can be powerful and Jesus's example clearly illustrates His divine power, Jesus's silence throughout the events leading to His eventual crucifixion was a powerful reminder of His mission on earth. While we would all get angry and fight back at all the lies, the accusation, and the mistreatment, Jesus stood silent to fulfill the path He had been chosen to walk. Jesus's life, words, and His silence mark extraordinary examples of the greatest leader in history.

The Art of Storytelling—Modern Parables

Jesus Christ was the master storyteller and communicator. One of his most effective communication tools was the parable. There are thirty-eight parables in the Gospels of Matthew, Mark, and Luke, and each of the parables tells a story in a simple, relatable, and memorable way that illustrates key points that Christ was trying to make at the time. The Gospel according to John, with one exception (the feeding of the five thousand), does not really include parables. Instead, John offers what might be described as long stories that illustrate broader issues. Whether you call it a parable or a long story, these narratives provoke, evoke, and challenge us to look at our own values and lives and see the world in a fundamentally different way. Through their nuanced simplicity, they provide answers we have always known but perhaps have not previously thought about or acknowledged. Christ was speaking to the common person and going toe-to-toe with doctrine and the religious leaders of time. He came with a message that could be appreciated and understood. People related to the message. And these messages translate very well to contemporary times.

One of my favorite ways to start a presentation about the social determinants of health is to tell the story of the "five most important numbers." The story goes a little like this. There is a young couple who recently found out they were pregnant. They go for their first trip to the doctor's office, and the staff welcomes the couple warmly. They have a pleasant discussion while the staff reviews the young mother-to-be's medical record. Going quiet, the assistant says the doctor will be in shortly to speak with them. The couple sits in silence, both looking anxiously at each other. After what seems like an eternity, the obstetrician walks in, introduces herself, and after some pleasantries, she pulls up a stool next to them and says, "I am worried about your diagnosis. Unfortunately, you are a code 43604." The young couple is confused; everything seemed to be going so well. They have no idea what a code 43604 is and ask the doctor to explain. She says, "That is your zip code."

The point of this story is that your health and well-being are more influenced by where you live than by your DNA. The story is a dramatic way to begin a discussion about the importance of social determinants. That, to me, is a kind of modern-day parable.

Recently, I heard a speaker discuss how a story can be much more powerful than facts. We have lots of examples, where we knew certain things from data, sometimes decades of data, but then a powerful story comes along, and that changes everything.

Think Not about What the Stories Say but What They Mean—And How to Act

When you are reading the parables and thinking about them, sometimes it is better to think less about what they say and more about what they mean, and then even more about what they can do. We should apply the same logic when we are thinking about how we tell stories and build the narrative for our organizations or even in our lives.

The parable about the sheep and the goat (Matthew 25:31–46) is more than about how a shepherd separates the sheep from the goats. It is about servant leadership: "Truly I tell you, whatever you did for one of the least of these brothers and sisters of mine, you did for me." And the opposite of that, "Truly I tell you, whatever you did not do for one of the least of these, you did not do for me." For those who provide food for the hungry, water for the thirsty, or clothes for someone in need are doing good. And those not doing those things will see eternal punishment.

In this way, the stories Christ told, and those that you tell, help force people to make a choice and act accordingly. In the parable about the sheep and goats, it is clear your priority is to behave as a servant leader.

Principles of Communication for Christian Leaders (or Non-Christian Leaders for That Matter)

Simplify, Simplify, Simplify

Christ understood the audience he was talking to, and he worked hard to simplify messages, whether that was with parables or longer discourses. While I was in Michigan, I worked with a CFO, one of the best CFOs I have worked with over the years, who could explain the economics of health care by using a dollar as the symbol. If you have a dollar of revenue, here is where our expenses go, and here is where we have to put dollars away because of depreciation. He was great at taking these complex issues and simplifying them.

Another really good boss I had believed you could take the most complex issue and simplify it by putting the information on a 2 X 2 chart. I would do a very detailed analysis for him, and he would say, "Great. Now do a two-by-two for me that you could use to explain this idea to one of our employees or a board member quickly." It was about taking complex issues and simplifying them. When you begin to do this, it almost becomes a checklist in your head about how to communicate and persuade people. If you can't put a plan on a page, it is too complex for people to understand. In the same way, Christ took the most complex issues and used a parable to illustrate the examples to use in life.

The Challenge in Storytelling and Stories— Exploring the Question "So What?"

When working with communications professionals on publicizing key programs we are creating to local, regional, or national audiences, they apply several different tests in determining how newsworthy a story is. They simply ask the question, "So what?" When we are focusing on social determinants of health programming, we ask the same question. What are we doing to improve the health and well-being of our communities? Making an impact relative to health disparities and health equity in this country is not about any theology or religion. It is about action.

Of course, how you answer the "So what?" test will be different from audience to audience, from community to community. Everything is situational. But if you ask this simple question, you can cut through a lot of clutter in your decision-making process.

Appreciate the Music of Words

It is not just the meaning in words and sentences. There is a rhythm and tempo to how the words are used. Many musicians have often been quoted as saying something like "Music is what happens between the notes." "Music is not in the notes, but in the silence between the notes."[1]

Christ, Matthew, Luke, Mark, and John all understood the importance of inspiring action through the music of words.

Repeating messages with frequency is one way to increase the power of words. Communications people often have a number of clever ways to explain things. One way to explain the importance of repeating a message is that "When you are getting really sick of hearing or telling a particular message, that is about the time your audience will just be starting to hear and understand the message." Christ repeated phrases, messages, stories, and other content all the time.

Mark, Matthew, Luke, and John all recognized the importance and power of repetition in writing the Gospels. For example, the story about the feeding of the five thousand is in all four Gospels, and it is a great story. We, as Christian leaders, should follow that lead and do the same. There are stories I tell all the time, like the "Zip Code 43604" story I mentioned earlier in this chapter. Sometimes I even repeat it to audiences who have heard the story before. You never know when someone will be ready to accept and understand the message you are delivering, and the story suddenly clicks and makes sense.

The synoptic Gospels of Mark, Matthew, and Luke often tell the same stories about Christ, but they tell them in slightly different ways, depending on the point they want to make or the context of what is happening at the time. The idea is that when something was said three times in scripture, if you say it once, it is important, if it is said twice, it is really important, and if it is said a third time, you really better not forget it.

There are certain themes Christ drove home, and then he drove home some more, and then he drove home even more. The old adage is true: first I am going to tell you what I am going to tell you, then I am going to tell you, and then I am going to tell you what I told you.

One way to make messages memorable is to use what is called parallel construction or repeated words and phrases that serve to emphasize key points. Christ and the writers of the Gospels were masters of this technique. For example, Christ would begin phrases and statements using "Woe to" or "I am." Using these words at the beginning of each phrase emphasizes its importance and makes it easier to understand what is being said.

Even the phrasing that Jesus used is critical. For example, saying the word *amen* just prior to making an important statement is a cue, a kind of verbal punctuation, that lets the listener know they should tune in to the message.

Another communication technique Christ used throughout the Gospels was inverting statements to make them more memorable. For example, in Mark, Christ says, "With men it is impossible, but not with God; for all things are possible with God." In Luke's version, the statement is "What is impossible with men is possible with God." This technique creates memorability.

Consider Other Points of View

When you are making decisions that impact people's lives, which happens every day in health care and particularly with major decisions, it is critical to consider each audience, listen, and bring them along where they are at. That is a challenge when you are advocating for a particular program or issue, but it is a process you have to go through.

It is pretty much a given today that many people tend to be skeptical about what motivates any given individual or organization. And in some cases, sometimes you just have to keep your head down and move forward. But as an organization, we always want to consider other people's points of view and make changes to plans based on feedback we receive. But like Christ's example, there are times when you listen, have compassion, but move ahead with purpose.

Several years ago, our organizational leadership, with our board's approval, made the decision to move all our corporate employees from offices all around a suburban metropolitan area to one campus in a downtown city core, which was bordered on the east end by a river. The net result would be an influx of several thousands of people from the suburbs to the central core of the city, an increase of people who hadn't been seen in decades. We had multiple options in bringing all our corporate employees together in one campus location, including having one major site in a suburb. But as part of our commitment to addressing the social determinants of health, which included a commitment to revitalization of a downtown area that had been decimated over the decades after a peak in the 1970s, we made the decision to move downtown. Part of that decision was to renovate and expand an old steam plant on a riverfront that had been vacant for decades. The renovation was more expensive than building in a suburb, but in the long term, we felt moving downtown was the right decision.

One of the key aspects of the renovation of the steam plant was what we had planned to do with a park that was right next to the steam plant. In its heyday, this park was a vibrant part of a waterfront that the public thoroughly enjoyed, with events and activities planned on a regular basis. But over the years, it was run down, and there were safety concerns about even being at the park. There were also some historic structures at the park—for example, a kiosk that had been brought from France to help give the park a European flair—that were in disrepair but needed to be preserved.

We created and implemented an extensive communication process that ensured we engaged the people who were invested in the park emotionally and provided them with details about how we would maintain the integrity of the park and its view to the river, while not only renovating the steam plant but building a parking lot for our employees. The parking lot was going to be partially underground, but there were going to be several levels above ground. We made multiple improvements to the park, including adding an outdoor sculpture that was made from parts of one of the steam plant's towers that had to be removed during construction, and installing a water feature for children and adults to enjoy.

We listened to the issues raised by concerned citizens and city representatives, and we made changes to our plans based on those concerns. While there were some bumps along the way, the community at large was very accepting of the move downtown, and six years later, the park is once again a destination for people to come to year-round. But we were up front in our communications for all our publics. We listened, we made changes based on those suggestions, and we turned public opinion into a positive for the community and for our organization. In fact, many of the people who initially opposed the renovation of the steam plant and park attended our first Party in the Park musical event downtown, clapping their hands, stamping their feet, and having a great time with the rest of the community who attended. Don't get me wrong. There was an initial negative reaction, and, of course, there are still people who complain, but there is overwhelming support now for what we did. I am always amazed by those who live to create controversy, bask in negative commentary, and seemingly use such experiences to foster negative attitudes and promote disharmony. But as we see through scripture, these people have and will always exist.

The Importance of Framing a Story—No Spin

When talking to people, they know you are probably advocating for a certain position. But communications professionals will tell you not to spin a story. Because when you spin anything, it creates its own vortex, like a tornado, and people can get hurt.

At another organization I worked for previously, there was a controversial parking project that we were undertaking. The reporter from one of the local news organizations covering the story lived in the same area as the hospital I worked at, and we occasionally ran into each other. He admitted to me that he was biased but that he was still going to do everything he could to defeat the project because he was personally very against it. When I reminded him that he was a journalist and that he was supposed to be unbiased, he told me flatly that he didn't care. Journalists don't really do themselves any favors when they say they are unbiased, because of course they are; they are human beings just like the rest of us—as are the editors who review and change stories, as are the publishers. They all have their points of view. But when they begin to insert their own personal agenda, that is when the credibility of the media suffers. In the last several years, our nation's media has done little to prove itself credible, but like the religious leaders of Christ's day, sometimes they love to wrap themselves in the robes of being a "journalist." To me, it is better to be honest that you are advocating for a position but to never lie about something. Because that will come back to bite you.

Christ certainly understood the importance of how to think through a message or how to frame a message. The Pharisees would often try to trap him into saying things or doing things that were against the rule of law. Christ would expertly turn the trap against the authorities of the time.

Communicate with People at Their Level

Christ communicated with people at their level, and depending on where they were at, he adapted his approach. He challenged the religious leaders, and even though he challenged them, the Pharisees and Sadducees were amazed at his skills. For those who were early in their faith, he kept things relatively simple. When he was in a crowd, he understood where they were at, so he knew what the message should be. He was always aware.

These are the same things we still do today. As an organization, when we were about to announce a decision, we looked at all the different publics that might be impacted by that decision and worked to communicate in a way that helped people understand what the decision is all about. Something that is a positive thing to one group of people may very well have a not so positive impact on another group of people. You are always balancing how you communicate.

For example, like many companies, we had management and employee town hall meetings. And you had to think through where these people were at because they were all at different levels. We took time to think about their work life, their fears, and what their space was at home, and what they were facing as we thought about how we communicated.

Say Thank You—A Lot

Small things make a difference. In health care, it is critically important to thank caregivers, because they are working twenty-four seven to heal, they work every holiday, and they take care of people who are nice and people you wouldn't let in your dining room. I try to always post thank yous to caregivers on my social media accounts, and invariably I will get back hundreds of responses from people thanking me for recognizing their work. You really can find enough ways to say thank you to others.

Action Should Come out of the Story

As a Christian leader, your vision should be broad based and should extend the scope of any institution, whether that is a corporate organization, or a church, or even a particular religion. Churches and religions offer structure, rituals, rules, and systems that we create as humans to maintain and manage authority. Your vision should rise above that, and your storytelling should reflect that. It is easy to argue fine points of theology (which means "speech about God") and doctrine, but there should be action that comes out of that theology and storytelling. Your narrative should help people rather than create an environment where they feel they have to go it alone. It should anticipate the questions of those looking for answers to important questions.

Who We Are Inside Will Be Revealed by Our Words and Actions

Words matter. Who we are inside will be revealed by our actions at some point. Mark, Luke, and Matthew all express this sentiment a little differently, but the concept is the same.

"A good man brings good things out of the good stored up in his heart, and an evil man brings evil things out of the evil stored up in his heart. The mouth speaks what the heart is full of" (Luke 6:45).

Matthew is angrier in how he expresses the point: "You brood of vipers, how can you who are evil say anything good? For the mouth speaks what the heart is full of" (Matthew 12:34).

Mark provides a few specific examples, saying, "For is it is from within, out of person's heart, that thoughts come—sexual immorality, theft, murder, adultery, greed, … All these evils come from inside and defile a person" (Mark 7:21–23).

As a Christian leader, the degree to which we walk closely with Jesus, the more our words will be evidence that we follow him and that we are true to our actions. The Holy Spirit will help us in being thoughtful, gracious, and true. For any leader, we know that who we are inside will ultimately be known through our words and actions. People are smart. They can immediately detect insincerity or a lack of integrity, which will ultimately destroy your credibility and trust among those following you.

Have the Long View When Spreading the Good Word

People I know in the health care industry sometimes come up to me and talk about the good media coverage we got in industry publications, particularly about what we were doing to address social determinants. The truth was we had been talking about and doing things to help address social determinants well before most health care organizations in this country. But it took years to build the story. We expanded the story, focusing on the personal determinants of health as well as social determinants. The layers kept being added. Just when you think that perhaps we had peaked with this issue, something else makes itself known, and we continued to expand. Christ, of course, only had three years, but through his death and resurrection, his disciples, the Gospels, and other techniques, he was able to extend the message throughout written history.

Anticipate Issues

One of the things organizational leaders need to be skilled at today is having the ability to anticipate issues, understand how they might impact the reputation of the organization, and then think through communications that will help influence outcomes. Christ was an expert at anticipating issues. Oftentimes, he mentioned to the disciples, "My time has not yet come," as he anticipated the anxiety of his followers and wanted to reassure them that everything was under control and that his time would come, but not just yet. He knew when to push and when to retreat. He knew when things would get out of hand, and he avoided these times when he needed to.

He was careful about the timing of the miracles he performed, anticipating the reaction of the public and leaders of the day. He had a clear path for when he communicated, how he communicated, and to whom he communicated. He anticipated when trouble was around, and he knew when to push and when to hold back. The impact he had over his three-year ministry infuriated the entire religious leadership of the day. And he stayed clear of the Romans. He set the stage carefully for his execution and resurrection and managed the situation by telling his disciples his death was near and that he would be resurrected. Had he remained silent during these times, the immediate and long-term impact of his life and death might have been minimized.

In a Crisis, Be Authentic—And Tell the Truth

Because of the nature of health care and health and well-being, We were always interacting with people and basically asking people for permission to do things to them. Even in the most positive decisions, we have to consider potential issues that might arise. At times, there are moments of crisis where there has been a negative outcome, or something negative has happened, and we need to communicate to a broad audience. In those moments, we try to own the issue, apologize if we have somehow injured someone, tell them how we are going to correct the issue, and then correct it. By our actions, we maintain or even build credibility and trust. It's also true with managers and board members. In times of crisis, you see every reaction. Some panic, some are paralyzed, some retreat and are not supportive, and others dig in to help.

The crisis for Christ was different. It was like how he communicated to people at critical junctures, especially toward the end of his life. His death and resurrection are a perfect example of crisis communication. He told people what was to come, several times, and then reassured people that good things would happen after his death, and good things did happen. He was in the middle of the ultimate crisis, but he conducted himself with great integrity throughout.

Relationships May Matter More

Be a Serial Networker

Many times as we are chasing a new project or investigating a new idea, we find that often it is the second or third contact we make who is the best person to help us in potentially partnering on a particular project. It requires constantly networking, in essence being a serial networker. Christ was a serial networker, walking among the crowd, talking and teaching and leading. There were no microphones or loudspeakers to carry Christ's words to the people. He had no choice but to be among the people. As a result, by nature, he had to be a serial networker.

We have forgotten some of that, and we need to get back to it. That is how we move through life. We walk through our crowds, the people we work with, praying and using the opportunities to communicate and network with others. I have been criticized by past bosses and others for meeting with too many people. Their verbal and nonverbal reaction was: "Why are you meeting with them? What a waste of time and energy."

The team I worked with has had many significant achievements related to social determinants over the last decade. The tendency for some may be to take a break and celebrate the good work, then pause and stop. But in many ways, the good work never stops. There is always a sense of urgency. You are always working toward what's next.

And sometimes good fortune is a bit of serendipity.

The organization recently signed a partnership with a high-tech company in California called Bitwise, which we worked with to purchase and then renovate an old worn-out building in Toledo's downtown core that had at one time been the main downtown post office.

One of our executives is a graduate of a college of engineering. She was at a conference for her alumni group, and the woman who spoke at the conference had a fascinating story. Irma L. Olguin Jr. was a daughter of field workers from one of the poorest areas of California. She was good at school and through a fortunate series of events found herself at the University of Toledo, graduating with a degree in computer science. After, she went back to California and became the cofounder and CEO of a tech company in Fresno called Bitwise. She had always told her folks that someday she would come back to Toledo because the city had always been good to her. Intrigued by the story, our executive connected with her after the presentation and talked to her. It turned out Bitwise was looking to partner with a number of other cities about the size of Toledo to establish an Innovation Center to train people to hold tech-related jobs, with a focus on women, minorities, LBGTQ, and migrants, adding hundreds of jobs to the work force in these cities.

Bitwise is a big software company. It provides an opportunity for nontraditional individuals in tech who might not otherwise have these opportunities, and they get really good jobs. Several businesses in our community are financial supporting Bitwise in our endeavor. Projects like these then parlay themselves into other opportunities, and you just keep building the momentum. Bitwise would not have happened without serial networking.

It is an interesting life lesson. When we were first talking about screening for the social determinants of health, we wanted to build our own IT tools. When we first were considering the idea, our IT leadership suggested that perhaps we should work with a large health care IT company and use existing technology. In the end, we created our own screening tool partnering with a new technology company. If we had stayed status quo, we wouldn't have a product we own and would not be able to do the things we can now do.

The easy path was to say we are going to continue to use the commercially available technology. We took the harder path and were capable of it. And we were rewarded.

What It Means to Be a Serial Networker

Someone actually called me a serial networker, and I started to think about it, and as I sometimes do, I started to noodle on piece of paper what being a serial network looks like. Here is what I came up with:

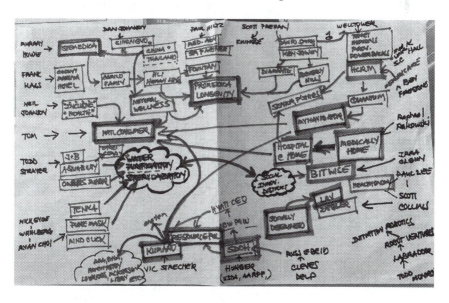

This only represents a small portion of the relationships that need to be built to achieve results, but I think it makes the point. You need to be willing to take the time to make the connections. It is the hard work of spreading the good word and building coalitions. It amazes me how many times it may be the second or third discussions that lead to powerful connections with others.

Stop Bowling Alone

I am a big fan of Robert Putnam, who wrote *Bowling Alone: The Collapse and Revival of American Community*, and a key takeaway from the book is that in our current culture, people don't know where to go to get support.[2] In

Bowling Alone, he outlines how we have isolated ourselves. We used to live our lives on our front porches and interact with our neighbors, but now the big porches are gone, and we are more isolated than ever, essentially bowling alone. In this era of social media, where there is constant commentary about everything and anything, we are more isolated than ever. It has changed our psyche and what we think is important in life. Putnam notes that while bowling numbers increased, leagues didn't. People were bowling alone. Gone were the social interactions where people came together, shared, and debated views and still remained friends.

As a Christian leader, you have to keep basic things in front of you. God created the earth; he sends his son to save us; but we still aren't equipped to deal with the world because we are all sinful—so he gave us the Holy Spirit. I pray every day to have the Holy Spirit direct my thoughts, direct the things I say today, and make sure I am a person of empathy. It is about how you approach the day and live these characteristics every single day.

One of my executives told the story about a retired brother who was very successful and got caught in a new lifestyle of retirement in a southern community. The man became caught up in the frenzy of a community wine auction, where bidding was $10,000 for a bottle of wine, competing against his friends and others. At that point, the wife leaned over to the husband and said, "We need to move back to the Midwest." And they did. It is so easy to get caught up in what people do and how they act. If you aren't constantly running that through a filter, it is easy to get trapped on a wide path.

Understand from the Other Person's Perspective

As part of our support of the Black Lives Matter movement, we had been having frank discussions with African American members of our leadership team that have proven to be intense and purposeful. What we heard is that as children, these black leaders were told by their parents things like, "When you go into certain grocery stores, you want to always be sure to take a shopping cart, even if you don't need one, because otherwise you could be accused of shoplifting." Or "You never go trick-or-treating with all black kids; you need to have a white kid." All of these cautions about growing up black in America. And I was wondering, *Why have we never talked about these things before?*

I grew up poor. I always thought that if you pick yourself up by your bootstraps, keep your head down, and work hard, good things will happen. But while I was poor, I wasn't a victim of racism or prejudice. And for people of color, working hard, getting an education, and keeping your head down often isn't enough.

Those who have opposed the Black Lives Matter movement often say that all lives matter. And while that is true, there is an entirely different set of systemic biases that people of color have to overcome—and that is what makes the movement necessary. The truth has been all lives don't matter in this country; black people and people of color are disadvantaged in so many ways. You have to call that out.

When I was at Case Western working on my doctorate, there was a black woman who was doing research on recidivism and black teens, and she said, "I am not concerned when my daughter brings home a black boy who went to prison; my concern is what prison they went to." How sad. For this black woman, hearing the story about a black male youth going to prison was almost accepted, and what was more important was which prison he went to, because some of the prisons were worse than others. That commentary is an indictment on the culture in our country. As Christian leaders, when we hear those things, we have to act compassionately—with an emphasis on *act*—to do something to change the culture of our communities and our country.

Another program we initiated was a series of fireside chat videos with our vice president and chief diversity, equity, and inclusion officer. In the video, we interviewed each other during two of the video chats. During the video chats, I talked about my mom. When I was younger and I would talk to her about someone in perhaps not the most positive manner, my mom would always say, "Do you know that person? Do you know their story? And if you don't, keep your mouth shut." She said this in a much nicer way, of course. Or she would say, "I didn't know you knew that person." And I would have to admit I didn't know them, and she would say, "Then why would you say you have an opinion?"

As leaders, and particularly as Christian leaders, we have to consider the points of views of others, no matter how painful the conversation. You need to really take time to think about things from the other person's perspective. That requires discipline and a willingness to really listen.

Currently, I am on the board of an art museum, and they focus on the discipline of visual literacy, and some of that can be applied to Christian leaders, and leaders in general, because it can enhance your ability to communicate and cultivate relationships. It is about an intensity of looking— really looking at minute details to think about what the artist may have meant in his or her work of art. All too often, people don't look and they don't listen because they are too focused on themselves and what they want to say. You need to get outside yourself. Christ was a tremendous listener who was able to get beyond himself to see other people's points of view.

By doing programs like the fireside chat, you begin to shift people's awareness and perception of the issue of BLM. You need to constantly be aware of the issues and keep them in front of you.

Bring People Along

Jesus spent a lot of time walking among the people as he brought them along. It was a ninety-eight mile walk between Nazareth and Bethlehem; ninety-nine miles from Jerusalem to Cana; and fourteen miles from Jerusalem to Samaria. He walked humbly among the people and brought them along as he moved from location to location. As Christian leaders, we should do the same. Get out as much as you can and walk with your employees and leaders. Bring them along as you meet and talk with them.

Cultivate Relationships through Compassion

When you think about cultivating relationships, a lot of people who are more traditional leaders don't get the idea of compassion. They don't understand the concept as to why Jesus would show compassion to sinners, sit down and eat with them, and care for them. You hear all the time how leaders begin to become unapproachable. I have always been a critic of organizations and associations that exist primarily to benefit executive leaders, which become affinity groups where the presidents talk about their position, money, and themselves. The question you want to ask them is, how much are they focused on the community? An executive in our community once asked me where I was from and where I went to school. He quickly dismissed someone from

Iowa (he actually said, "Can anything good come out of Iowa?") and noted that I had not gone to an Ivy League school.

Christ cultivated relationships by meeting people on their level, whether it was fishermen, the Samaritan woman, or others. He understood people, was compassionate, and displayed an incredible emotional intelligence with the capacity to be self-aware, self-regulating, internally motivated, and empathetic. He used examples and stories that people could relate to. He was compassionate to those who were sick, and he healed. Even in the interchange with the woman who touched his robe, he was very compassionate to her. Christ cared deeply for those who struggled. He helped the hungry to get food, helped the thirsty to get drink, helped the homeless to find a home, helped the one who had no clothes to get clothes, and helped the sick to find comfort. At the same time, he was vicious with the religious leaders of the day.

Compassion requires significant introspection and preparation. Some people are naturally very compassionate, and they want to save the world. For others, it is something they have learned that makes them compassionate. I look at a lot of the social determinants programs we have implemented over the years, and we have learned a lot; and as we have learned, we have done more.

I was on a webinar recently with the physician who runs a major health care organization. She was talking about the social needs of the poor in her region and how they needed to address those issues. I thought, *That conversation would never have happened five years ago.* So that compassion built into addressing the social determinants of health has led to an evolution of action not only within our organization but nationally. We have come a long way.

Part of being compassionate is to reflect on who you are and where you came from. Understand your frailties and failures and acknowledge that you are an incomplete leader. You have to have a realistic view of yourself. I am always amazed by people, because all too often, they view things through an "it's all about me" lens. You have to cut people some slack, but when you listen to people talk sometimes, you wonder, *Is it really all about them?* And for certain people, it is. Not that they can't be compassionate, but the more egotistical, narcissistic you are, the less you tend to be compassionate.

You have to have a realistic view of yourself. We really are just not that good.

Communicate with Focus and Clarity

There are people who have unsurpassed focus and clarity, like a clear blue flame. They burn with a clear focus on what they are about and what they are trying to do. That was Christ, and that is what we are trying to do with people and their needs. And his disciples ultimately burned with the clear focus also in spreading the word.

Be Sure to Celebrate

All good leaders find time to celebrate. Christ certainly did. Because he understood that ultimately, to create change and move things along, he had to establish connections and relationships with people. For us, that means sometimes you take your leaders out for a beer when you want to informally coach them and talk one to one so the person you are coaching understands you are interested in them and their careers.

And it means being prepared to socialize and network at large gatherings. When we are at big parties, I tell my wife, "Well, time to go to work," because that is what it is sometimes. You need to build relationships, and big gatherings like that help do that. It is work for me to do that, and that is okay.

Walking the Narrow Path and Seeking an Expansive Perspective

In thinking again of the parables, because of the nature of how they were told and then written by the disciples, and because of the nature of words themselves, the parables go beyond the literal to broader interpretations. In this way, they illustrate the narrow path but allow for a broader view of things. The narrow path should never be thought of as a negative but as one more of faith, of discipline, and about looking for meaning in the example, the life, and the resurrection of our Lord, Jesus Christ.

You have to be open to change and interpretation. That is the nature of faith. The Christian leader as communicator has to take a step back from the world while walking that narrow path. Follow the narrow path, but do not take the narrow, literal view all the time. We need to seek a broader view while taking that narrow path. It is good to ask questions and challenge yourself and others.

You don't walk alone. You have the Holy Spirit to help guide you and guard your heart and mind. The Holy Spirit can serve as a source of strength that can help galvanize your thoughts as you make decisions and communicate about them. It is your frame of reference and helps provide perspective, which is our next chapter.

TWELVE

GAINING AND MAINTAINING PERSPECTIVE

My wife, Barbara, and I both grew up in northwest Iowa. My home was in a town called Sioux Center, between Sioux City and Sioux Falls, South Dakota, and Barbara grew up on a farm near Boyden. Her family had one of these hundred-year family farms that her father worked, and now her brothers work it. We both went to the same small church college of about a thousand students, called Northwestern College in Orange City, Iowa, but we never met there. Northwestern is a college of the Reformed Church of America. I jokingly say I hung out with all the academic types, while she hung out with the party people (just kidding). We were in different classes and had different majors, so we never met or talked. I actually lived with her cousin for a while, but we still didn't meet. It was about five years later, after college, we both happened to be in a church back in Iowa one night. We ran into each other and acknowledged that we looked familiar to each other. We went out, and six weeks later, we were engaged. We got married about ten months later.

We just had that immediate connection. We had the same upbringing, faith, and aspirations. And forty years later, we still have that same connection. I have been so blessed to have found someone like Barbara. She has been my rock for so many years, and it is from her that I have oftentimes found perspective. She is so grounded in her faith and how she lives her life. It is remarkable. And I get tremendous strength from that perspective.

For those not as fortunate to have married someone with that sound, fundamental base, there are ways that Christian leaders can maintain and gain perspective throughout life.

Joy from Becoming a More Complete Leader

We are all incomplete leaders; we all are flawed; we all are imperfect; we are all sinful. To be a more complete Christian leader, you can look to John 16:24 for support. It is Christ who completes us: "Until now you have not asked for anything in my name. Ask and you will receive, and your joy will be complete." The complete leader is the one who follows the Beatitudes, is humble, is constantly seeking to grow, pays attention to others, and follows the principles of Christ's leadership. When we are solidly following Christ's leadership and applying that leadership approach to his life, that is when we are the most complete leader we can be. Over my career, I have been in numerous social situations that can best be described as secular noise. Don't get me wrong. I like the second glass of wine as much as anybody, but the social noise in the life of a leader can be strikingly uncomfortable.

The word *joy* in the verse from John is an interesting one, because joy can often come from a challenging situation or one that had been filled with grief. I am always amazed that when we are talking about an issue or a tough decision or issue, in the aftermath, we often talk about it joyfully because through the hard times, we have found tremendous growth. You might be saddened because of the situation, but on the other hand, tremendous opportunity comes from those difficult moments. We become more complete leaders, we become more empathetic, we become better listeners. It becomes who we are.

Gaining Perspective Requires Preparedness and Patience

My experience in church is that no one talked about leadership. There was no discussion about how you could apply your Sunday life to work. They shouldn't be two separate worlds, but there was nothing to bridge the gap. Because of that, you are often left to think through the path of your life on your own, what you take on that road to help you get where you are going, and what that path means to you. Creating that connection between Christ's leadership example and what we do every day, whether it is work ethic or leadership style, is how you bring perspective in life. It is not revolutionary, but it is just not often taught or thought about. That means you have to be more diligent, you have to prepare, and you have to watch constantly. Faith is not celebrated in most companies today, and even talking about your faith is not only discouraged but, in some instances, may end or derail your career. So how did this happen?

Because we are bombarded with information, misinformation, and disinformation, faith is not cultivated during a crisis but before a crisis happens, during ordinary days. You fall back on your faith when things are hard, because it defines who you are and what you practice. You have to have that underpinning.

In the introduction of this book, we talked about the Dutch reformation concept called TULIP (total depravity, unconditional election, limited atonement, irresistible grace, and preservation of the saints). Barbara and I also grew up with the Five Solas, which were established during the Protestant Reformation as principles to live by. The Five Solas are: Sola Scriptura (scripture alone), Sola Fide (faith alone), Sola Gratia (grace alone), Solus Christus (Christ alone), and Soli Deo Gloria (to the glory of God alone). And like TULIP, you may or may not totally agree with every aspect of the Solas, but they can serve as a foundation for our life's view. For example, the first Sola talks about how the scriptures are a trustworthy authority for faith. That doesn't mean that the Bible is the only place where you will find truth, but it will serve as a framework for your belief and values system. Every day, we step off the narrow path. Revisiting our framework can help clarify our purpose. This helps bring us back to the path. They are tools for us to use in life. We live by relying on our faith, based on the scriptures, focused on Christ, saved by grace (nothing we deserved), and giving glory to our God! Pretty powerful stuff!

The Long Way

The shortest way isn't always the best. This is where being prepared is important. Sometimes you have to be patient because God may take you on a different route altogether. And in this culture of immediate gratification, if you don't get something right away, something is wrong. The narrow road may be the longer road. It may be a different perspective than the world, so it may be harder. It may take more work and preparation, where the wide road may be the quickest and the easiest, filled with shiny objects. The narrow road is really the road of Christ, the road of God, and the wide road is the road of the world. You have to prepare for that challenge every day, every hour, every minute, every second.

Having Perspective with Challenging Bosses

As I mentioned earlier, I have worked for several challenging bosses over the years. You end up praying a lot, thinking a lot about leadership from a Christian perspective, or in some instances, trying not to think about it at all! When you think about working for leaders who were not Christian in their actions, it does make you look back at your own faith and your own leadership style. In that case, you learn not so much what to do but what not to do. When you experience that in life, it reinforces the principles and values that Christ taught and led by and how we are to treat people.

It is a process of growth as well as just plowing through the day at work. At times, with some of the challenging bosses, I thought about switching careers or just taking a different job. But when you think about it from a Christian perspective, you know you are going to always have these situations. With one boss, I was considering taking a job in Wisconsin and commuting to and from my current home so as to not uproot the family. Just as I was in Wisconsin getting ready for a final interview for that job, I was thinking about one of my sons who was involved in sports. I was anxious to get home, but my flight was delayed and I got stuck in Wisconsin, so I missed the game. And I thought, *I can't do this for two years while the kids grow up.* I didn't take the job. I remember thinking about feeling trapped and then becoming even more determined to survive!

Perspective Is Not Either/or—It Is Yes/And

The news these days is so polarized it is hard to know which media outlet actual offers any factual news. You don't want to use either the alt-left media or the alt-right to gain perspective. Some of the ultraright conservatives justify personal agendas through scripture. Some of the ultraleft liberals, elitist people who say they are the most "tolerant," are in fact some of the least tolerant people you will find if you don't agree with them. So on the Far Right or Far Left, there are challenges. Over the last several years, I have found myself listening less to news, not reading newspapers, and refusing to read comments on social media.

One of the challenges with today's media environment is that, increasingly, algorithms determine what we hear and see, and the news outlets only feed you what you want to hear. It is the strength of weak ties on steroids. As a result, we are becoming even more isolated inside our own belief silos. Because what we hear just keeps reaffirming that we have the answer, and no one else can have a point of view. As a result, we become incredibly intolerant of one another.

Christ wasn't a Democrat, he wasn't a Republican, and he wasn't an independent; he wasn't a conservative or a liberal. For Christians, it cannot be either/or. It is more like yes/and. Christian values cut across all parties. Christ tended to those in need, not to those in positions of power. Many Christians today would be similarly bothered by who Christ talked to, associated with, and embraced. He came for the sinners and those most in need. He hung out with people whose lives were less than pure and many who we would hesitate to welcome into our homes.

It is not ours to judge or be the avenger. We need to listen to other points of view. The adage that *as we get older, we know less* is so true. I was mistakenly pretty confident that I knew more when I was younger. Today, I try to judge less and accept more. While I may believe that some actions are sinful, I also know that we all do many, many things that Christ would find just as sinful. Christ would look at someone we would condemn and say, "Sin no more."

Principles to Help Gain Perspective

In thinking through how to gain and maintain perspective in life and in leadership, there is a series of processes and activities to consider. What follows are ten things for gaining and maintaining perspective.

1. Prayer: The Powerful Tool to Gain Perspective

Prayer is one of the key ways I am able to achieve perspective. Today, my prayer life is better than it has been at any time in my life. That said, while it is better, I still need to improve. We all need the peace of God.

Every time Christ faced an important decision or at critical moments, he went off to the mountain or another solitary place where he prayed. Examples where Christ prayed include: before he selected his disciples (Mark 1:35, Luke 6:12), at the transfiguration (Luke 9:28–31), and many others. I wish I could say I prayed before every major decision in my life, but I have done it increasingly as I have gotten older. I find myself increasingly praying for guidance. I pray to the Holy Spirit for his guidance and leadership. I am more conscious now about the blessings I have, the resources available to me, and the opportunities to make an impact, and I realize that I will be judged for the decisions I make. So I pray for the organization, and I pray that we do things right. As a leader of an organization, I really started to pray more often, and over the last couple of years, I have continued to increase my praying.

How to Pray

Jesus and the disciples give us guidance not only on the need to pray but also on how to pray. It is important to be humble and private in pray. As in Matthew 6:5–15, when you pray, go to a private space. And when you pray, don't be a hypocrite and pray in the public; don't babble on, because it is not about the length of the prayer but the quality of the prayer. Be respectful. It is all about what is motivating you to pray. Ultimately, it is about having a prayerful relationship with Christ.

When former president Trump took a Bible and held it up in front of a church for a photo op during a Black Lives Matter protest in Washington, DC, was that being humble, or was it a hypocritical attempt to take a powerful symbol and use it for his personal gain?

There is a need to be careful about how we use prayer. Prayer is not like creating your own spiritual whiteboard where you put all your individual requests for Christ and God to fulfill. This is not the prosperity Gospel where, if I pray it, God will bless you and make it happen like some kind of magic. We are quick to claim miracles and answered prayers to justify our behavior. But when these personal requests aren't granted, sometimes people get bitter. We want to make sure we think about the power of prayer and how we use it. We want to make sure we approach prayer through Christ's example. With that in mind, we can bring our requests. And God will guard our heart and mind.

As we become more disciplined with prayer, it will become as natural as breathing, a kind of spiritual breath. It will become like an ongoing conversation with God, how you start and end your day, and for the moments in between.

The Science of Prayer

Prayers are not all created equal. Research has suggested that when you approach God in prayer, mental health outcomes seem to be better, whereas if your prayer is angry, mental health outcomes were not as good.[1]

When I talked to Vic Strecher about prayer, he put prayer alongside meditation, and I kept telling him that it is completely different. People can get confused because some of the processes related to prayer and meditation can be similar. You want to aware of your breath, slow yourself down, and focus on something. A story by Elizabeth Bernstein in the *Wall Street Journal* reported on research indicating that people who meditated on the words "God is love" were getting a more positive reaction because of the connection to God.[2] When you think about that, the question becomes, do you have a more positive reaction because the idea of God makes you feel better, or is it because you are praying in a Godly matter? Christians would say of course it is, not because some study showed these results.

Vic is a scientist, so it is still true for him that he associates prayer and meditation as similar events. But I hope he is still pondering it. He has asked questions about how I feel about the importance of prayer and how it helps me. So he is perhaps a little more accepting that prayer is different for people.

2. Be Still

The remedy for distractions is the same now as it was in earlier and simpler times: prayer, meditation, and the cultivation of the inner life. Distractions must be conquered, or they will conquer us, so we want to cultivate simplicity, be still, and fill our minds and souls with the Word of God.

When you look at Christ's example as a leader, particularly when things got difficult or when he was facing decisions, he kept a very tight, small group, but he also escaped to stillness and to prayer. He went to his knees and prayed, and he poured his heart out. For all the psychological and mental health reasons you can think of, it is a great example of how we should live our lives.

My wife is a great example of the power of stillness. When we are home, I might have the television on, and Barbara could be at home all day and not even think about turning it on. She is very comfortable with silence and stillness. I always needed something on, whether it was television or music. Barbara would say to me, "How can you listen to that? It is really distracting," to which I would reply, "I'm not really listening. I just like having it on." I just need to have noise at times.

Through most of my life, when I am in a car going to work or somewhere, I tend to be listening to something, a podcast or radio. My wife, on the other hand, never turns on the radio. She is radio silent. And that was distracting to me. But I learned from that, and now increasingly I am doing the same thing. It allows you to get a little more focused on the day. It is uplifting to your heart and mind—that notion of silence and being in reverence. It all goes to your heart and how you look to Christ and respect for God. So be still and know God.

3. Stay Focused on God / Have a Strong Foundation

Having a strong foundation in life is critical. And it is not just listening but putting words in action. As Matthew says in 7:26–27, "But everyone who hears these words of mine and does not put them into practice is like a foolish man who built his house on sand. The rain came down, the streams rose, and the winds blew and beat against that house, and it fell with a great crash."

When you begin to think about the challenges in life and what you should rely on, everyone needs a strong foundation that will hold solid during those difficult times. Preparing for the narrow path, you need to walk slowly, carefully, and methodically and ensure that when you take a step forward, it is a sure step. We want to make sure those fundamental principles we step on are solid as rock. And that foundation is Christ. How did you build your leadership approach? Did you build your approach on the solid foundation of Christ's example, or did you build it on a wider path? The verse from Matthew is one of those great Bible verses that can apply in many ways. You should build your leadership approach on the foundation of Christ. You should build your marriage on the rock of Christ. You should build your life on the foundation of Christ's example and teaching. You should build up your children on the rock. It is just a great way to think about strong foundations in life.

It's hard when you think about leadership. There is no real leadership journal of Christ. What happens it that you are bombarded almost everywhere you look with non-Christian examples of leadership and life. Every year, you can review the leading business books, and rarely do you see a reference to faith. That is not to say that people who offer non-Christian examples aren't Christians. But it often can feel like everything is being proposed from a non-Christian lens. For some reason, Christians have not done enough to point leaders to Christ as the leadership example. In fact, most use secular books and wrap them in a Christian book cover. As long as you are a better leader, it is great for Christianity. As a result, you need to have that solid foundation, making sure you are constantly focused on it.

How do you do that? For starters, you can't just show up to work and wing it, just dealing with whatever as it is thrown at you. You have to prepare for the day. You prepare yourself by prayer or through scripture. Just the simple act of praying for your job and the people you work with and the organization you represent gives you an entirely different attitude about work and those you work with.

You want to try to surround yourself with people who help bring light to illuminate your path. They may well be people who disagree with you and have different points of view. That is the strength of weak ties. But they are people who share your heart, mind, and soul. They have your back. They are also people who follow a Christ-inspired leadership approach, whether or not they are Christian.

Many people know the widely quoted section of the verse from John 8:32, which says, "The truth will set you free." But fewer people are as familiar with the verse before it, which says, "To the Jews who had believed him, Jesus said, 'If you hold to my teaching, you are really my disciples. Then you will know the truth, and the truth will set you free.'" Truth comes from Christ's teaching and leadership example, and that is what we need to hold on to.

People will readily say, "The truth will set you free," but immediately after that, will either claim or imply that "And oh, by the way, the truth is what I just said. What I believe!" People use this partially quoted verse as a rationale for whatever cause or ideology they are espousing. These are people typically on the Far Left or the Far Right who are in their own way elitists who have no tolerance for what other people say. And if you disagree with them, then you do not know the truth.

But when you read the two sentences together, you have a better understanding of what Christ intended and maintain perspective. You find that there is no truth without God or God's Word. That leaves you directionless. The more you are with God's words, the easier it is to direct your thoughts. You have to have that foundation first and hold to Christ's teaching. Then you will be Christian leaders, you will know the truth, and that truth of the leadership example of Christ will set you free.

4. Depend on God—Give Up Control

Developing a constant and consistent belief and trust in Christ and God is necessary if you hope to model a Christian-based leadership style. For instance, before Jesus raised Lazarus from the dead, his faith in his Father demonstrated the power of God in what seemed a hopeless situation.

You build your faith in good times and bad. We grew up with a particular biblical framework for understanding what the Bible teaches us. This preparation about what we believe and how we look at things becomes our view of life. So much of faith and life comes from a biblical view of the world (or not) and God's role in your life (or not). For many people, it's not like that. To some, God is just an observer. This preparation has to happen early on, well before you are tested in life, because that preparation is the foundation for your daily routine, so that when a crisis does occur, you will manage it rather than have the crisis manage you.

When you pray, you give up control, admit your weakness, and ask for God's help. As a Christian leader, it is important to acknowledge that you are not the one totally in control.

5. Understand What's Important

Back in Jesus's day, there were many written and unwritten expectations regarding how to obey written laws and laws written well beyond what was in scripture. These rules put a heavy burden on those who sought to follow.

Jesus rejected these human-made rules, simplified things, and released people from the burden of the heavy yoke, as in Matthew 11:28–30, where he says, "Come to me, all you who are weary and burdened, and I will give you rest. Take my yoke upon you and learn from me, for I am gentle and humble in heart, and you will find rest for your souls. For my yoke is easy and my burden is light." Christians can be burdened today by trying to live a Christian life while also carrying the secular workplace at the same time.

The leaders during Christ's time created all these rules that had no biblical basis, yet they came up with human-made rules that Christ rejected and didn't follow. As you think about leadership, it is important to have a clear understanding in your own mind about what rules are from humans and which are from God. For example, when you look at some business leaders who create rules to fire the bottom 10 percent of performers each year, you won't find that anywhere in the leadership example of Christ. As you look at modern-day servant leadership approaches, you quickly realize that the foundation from that came from the Gospels and Christ's leadership example. And you want to say, "Yeah, man, Christ was the ultimate servant leader." The Gospels, the Sermon on the Mount, and the Beatitudes are places you can go to understand what is important and what your leadership approach should be. That is our starting point, not the top business leaders of our time. Among the challenges for leaders following Christ are the new rules that our secular society puts on modern leadership.

6. Truth Leads to Perspective

The Gospel of John focuses on the question of truth, while acknowledging that the law was given through Moses, that grace and truth come through Jesus, and that perhaps our actions reveal truth. Indeed, throughout the Gospel of John, Jesus interacts with those in positions of authority and power, and through their words and actions, they really challenge that any real truth exists. For example, during the interchange between Pilate and Christ in John 19:37–38, Jesus says, "I've come into the world for this: to give evidence about truth. Everyone who belongs to the truth listens to my voice." To which Pilate responds, "Truth. What's that?"

What is going on in our current environment illustrates how hard it can be at times to define exactly what truth is. What we view as truth seems more complicated, sophisticated, and more difficult to understand today. The message of Christ is more true and simple. The way social media works, you will receive a slanted view, and it is often hard to figure out truth and reality. For example, even Wikipedia can be a source for misinformation because, since it is open source, people can edit entries to suit their purpose or agenda. What is intended to help people understand what is going on in the world may no longer be a credible source. Having true interactions with people and debating issues with integrity has largely been lost.

The conversation between Jesus and Pilate foreshadows what is happening in our current environment as people make up their own truths to meet their needs. While Pilate found no reason to condemn Christ, he did so to appease the popular view of the day. If you step back from the craziness and step back to faith and what you believe in and how you believe you should conduct yourself, the world would be a better place.

You think about leadership today and the trappings of leadership, money, housing, cars, and title. I don't care who you are; after a while, you like it, and special treatment becomes the standard expectation. Christ was the opposite; he didn't seek this attention. He had no possessions, he didn't belong to clubs, and he walked and lived off the grid.

There are parts of the scripture that none of us will ever understand; there will be parts that will alienate. What makes some of those verses challenging is that it is difficult to understand the context of the time. To me, I have done things that I have done in life that I should be concerned about. God will be the final judge. It is not for us to say one way or the other.

To some of our political leaders today, it is hard to understand from one moment to the next what is truth. And for any Christian to feel they need to support a candidate because of their political affiliation, that just doesn't make sense. Christian faith gives you the background with how you should deal with situations when truth is not clear. You can only imagine what Christ would think of many of our political leaders today.

7. Leadership Equals Discipleship

You can be academically strong and a head learner, but there are a lot of people who are that way who aren't necessarily strong leaders. Some of the people I went to graduate school with were academically brilliant, and I thought at the time they would be superstars in their careers. But a number of them didn't have the stellar careers it seemed they would have. And it seems like a lot of that had to do with how they treated people in their careers and their ability to be compassionate and empathetic. Those softer skills like kindness, compassion, and humility often matter more than intellectual and technical skills. You need both to be a successful Christian leader.

The ability to lead with both the heart and the mind may be a difference between what makes up a strong manager and what qualities are needed to be a strong leader. A strong manager is often concerned with numbers, projects, and tasks, where leaders are much more about inspiration and vision. They have the ability to convince people to follow them; they have a mindset for what they want to do and how they want to do it.

As leaders, we are all called to be disciples of Christ. We are invited to take up the cross. And as we follow with mind, body, and soul, we gain perspective. That is a heavy burden.

As a Christian leader, this requires a mental shift away from the secular to the example of Christ. This verse from Philippians 4:8 says it well: "Finally, brothers and sisters, whatever is true, whatever is noble, whatever is right, whatever is pure, whatever is lovely, whatever is admirable—if anything is excellent or praiseworthy—think about such things." Finding the true, honorable, right, and pure requires discipline, a mental shift, and new habits.

In her book *Ragged: Spiritual Disciplines for the Spiritually Exhausted*, Gretchen Ronnevik identifies a number of holy-therapy exercises to help provide a foundation for us.[3] These exercises include, prayer, reading scripture, meditation, confession, generosity, and lament, among others. By taking a disciplined approach with these exercises, we are better able to deal with the hard questions life throws at us and have a better appreciation for the depth of faith God gives us.

8. Trust

To gain perspective is to fully trust God and Christ. Many people struggle with this for a variety of reasons: they may worry that they will lose control if they trust God; they may worry that trusting God could lead them to become religious zealots; they may feel guilty; they may worry what others think; they may feel it will restrict them. The truth is that none of these things will happen.

You can parallel that into what Christian leadership is and what Christian leadership should look like. The Bible gives us comfort in 1 John 4:16–18" "God is love ... There is no fear in love ... The one who fears is not made perfect in love." And, of course, God has given us the leadership example of Christ. And what I have found is that the more you trust in Christ, the less fear you feel.

Fame is fleeting, and you need to have resilience as a disciple. Rick Warren, a nationally recognized pastor who wrote a best-selling book, *The Purpose-Driven Life*, is a perfect example of being resilient.[4] After his book was published, he took on a celebrity status of sorts, and then tragically, his son died. Some began to rake him over the coals, questioning his authenticity, and they honestly were cruel to him. As so often happens in our culture, one minute people love you, and the next they are throwing stones at you. As a Christian leader and disciple, you have to not get too caught up when people praise you or when people criticize you.

In the book *Emotional intelligence*, Daniel Goleman talks about how the capacity to be in control, to be aware, and to be able to express your emotions is critical to achieving trust.[5] Those concepts can be taken right out of the Beatitudes. When you think about emotionally intelligent people having skills like empathy and listening, it is really about having people skills. The single most predictable factor of leadership failure is a lack of emotional intelligence. Rarely do you demote someone because they aren't competent. Demotions happen most often because of a lack of people skills. Christ was always very aware of his surroundings; he self-regulated, he had internal motivations, he was empathetic, and he had tremendous social skills.

You can picture Christ walking through the crowds, bantering with people, holding children, teaching, and then he is debating the people in the synagogue or throwing out the money changers. You think about the woman at the well: he listened to her, he talked to her, he gave her water, and he gave a message to sin no more. Having emotional intelligence doesn't mean you can get cranked up. It is about reading the situation and the people. In practice, so many people don't read the room. They don't ask questions. They are more interested in what they want to say next. They don't read nonverbals. Christ met people where they were at in life. He was kind, generous, and guiding to those in need and was forceful to those who tried to control and push others down and take advantage of people and situations.

Even though you may not be aware of it, God is with us even as we go about our daily routine. It is as simple or as challenging as a matter of trust.

9. Be Comfortable in How You Want to Measure Success

When I was younger, I worked for someone who advised me, "Get yourself in a position where you don't need the job." I never understood what he was saying when I was younger. But his point was, if you need the job, you are not always going to be free to do what you need to do. You need to be free to do the things you need to do and say the things you need to say.

While there is a financial aspect to this, there is a spiritual side also. I think my boss was focused on the financial side of things. Getting yourself in a financial position is important, but it is probably more important to think about getting yourself in the correct spiritual position to do the things you need to do.

My background and evolving focus on the narrow road always helped me to be able to be focused on the issue at hand. Parents of that generation were all about raising their children to keep their mouths shut, get a job, keep your head down, take care of your family, and don't think too much of yourself.

The focus should not be on end product but the quality of how you got to the end product. Some people are focused on outputs and not so much on outcomes. For some religious organizations, it is all about chasing numbers. We have put the world's metrics on our churches. The bigger the better is not necessarily the way to measure success.

It is important to not judge success by worldly measurements, such as wealth or status. You have to judge success based on the leadership example of Christ. There are many ways to measure success as a Christian leader. As a baseline measure, I try to approach work and life with the heart of a servant, stay humble, and each day strive to live the example of Christ through the Beatitudes and the Great Commandment.

Over the years in establishing and expanding how we address the social determinants of health at our organization, we have had many discussions about how to measure success, and we have a research division that helps us do that. For me, measurement starts with the blessings and opportunities you have been offered in life and how you have used them. And the outcome is the impact you have made based on those resources. With the social determinants, measurement is about the actions we have taken to address issues of health disparities and inequities. As a health care organization, we could have stayed on a purely clinical path. But instead, because of our resources and opportunities, we have been able to expand into social and personal factors that impact health and well-being, and we have been addressing these social determinants that lead to health disparities to improve health and well-being not only for the individual but for the community as well.

The government and the community are all clamoring for numbers that measure the success of addressing health disparities. You can get wrapped up in that. Health and well-being outcomes as we address these health disparities in some instances is tough to measure in the short term. Some areas, like access to food and hunger disparities, are easier to measure in the short term. We have been able to show, for example, that reducing food insecurity can reduce readmissions to hospitals and reduce usages of emergency departments, which are very expensive. But other issues, like housing, education, and financial security can take much longer, perhaps even generations, to really determine outcomes. That means you have to be committed to moving forward and measure immediate successes, knowing that your actions will lead to greater positive community and individual outcomes.

We think a lot about how to address systemic racism in this country. And there are things we can do in the short term to move things forward. But issues like generational poverty, where you may not see an immediate result, are perhaps even more important to address, although it may take generations to measure. It is our inclination to put a metric around everything. But sometimes you have to put numbers aside, trust your faith, and act.

10. Let the Holy Spirit Be Your Guide

Leadership can be lonely. As a CEO, from whom do you receive affirmation? You won't necessarily get it from a board of directors. You have people around you telling you mostly positive things. Then you go home, and it is sometimes hard to explain what you do. One place for affirmation is the Holy Spirit.

Increasingly, as I get older, I pray to and ask the Holy Spirit for guidance. I also find myself spending more time listening to the Holy Spirit. I know that to some that may sound a little out there, but once you accept the Holy Spirit, nothing is more natural. That doesn't mean I am actually listening to the spoken words of the Holy Spirit. It is more like an urging. I know when my spiritual life is really good that the decisions I am making are in line with the urging of the Holy Spirit—and I feel good. There is a greater sense that what I am doing is right. There is a sense that I am walking with God. Thinking back, I wish I would have thought more about listening to the Holy Spirit, because now my confidence comes from the Holy Spirit. Some may say this sounds mystical, and some might say it is my conscience. Yet it is true.

Relying on the Holy Spirit gives you a sense of peace. It is very calming. It helps you feel like you are not alone.

I am here to emulate Christ as best I can as a simple person with the power of the Holy Spirit. And I am going to start by concentrating on my love of Christ, thankfulness for salvation, and the command to live the life we should live and to treat people with the same respect and caring that Christ did. When you think about that every day, you pray it, and you open yourself and pray to the Holy Spirit for guidance, it starts to impact on your mind and softens your heart in a positive way.

Doctrine is buoyed by the Holy Spirit. Your words, your decisions, and how you process decisions all use the moral compass of the Holy Spirit.

First Corinthians 2:10–12 shows us the qualities of Christ-centered leaders: "These are the things God has revealed to us by his Spirit. The Spirit searches all things, even the deep things of God. For who knows a person's thoughts except their own spirit within them? In the same way no one knows the thoughts of God except the Spirit of God. What we have received is not the spirit of the world, but the Spirit who is from God, so that we may understand what God has freely given us."

I look back at my life and feel better than I did five years ago, but I still question if I have a total commitment to Christ. Am I to the point I should be in following the example of Christ? We are sinful and incomplete. You can get down and will never quite be to the point you want to be, but you keep growing, moving in the right direction. Wherever you are at in life, there will always be change. Whether you are a twenty-year-old leader or an eighty-year-old leader, it is that constant pursuit to grow and get better. Don't have a fixed mindset. Always question. Always learn. Always strive to be better. Then your Christian faith guided by the Holy Spirit will have an opportunity to shine.

THIRTEEN

TOWARD A CHRIST-INSPIRED LEADERSHIP APPROACH

My life, along with my wife's, has been a journey from a family and community based heavily in doctrine to a secular world and many different types of organized religions. Through that journey, I have developed a Christian framework that helps me as a leader in business and in the community and through life as we strive to be better spouses, parents, mentors, children, siblings, partners, employers, citizens—and, most importantly, better men and women of faith. I believe everyone should develop their own framework to help them navigate through their work life. It may be Bible based or based on a different framework, but there should be a foundation to help think about and move forward in meeting the challenges that face us all.

The five key principles of my Christ-inspired approach follow:

1. Frame Up Your Mind and Soul

We are simple, flawed people. That is our nature. It is important to frame our mind to help keep our hearts and minds on a narrow path focused on servant leadership.

This is a process that continues to build over time. As I have gotten older, I have found it increasingly important to take time every day to reflect on how Jesus led and strive to apply his approach in my daily life. That's where Jesus lived!

Prayer is one way to do that, and the Bible tells us to bring everything in prayer. A common structure you can use to gain perspective through prayers is abbreviated to the acronym ACTS: adoration; confession of your sins; thanks to God; and supplication.[1] Then you make your requests.

Prayer can really bring peace of mind, create a sense of purpose, and strengthen you in life. Prayer on a daily basis takes discipline, and for busy people, that can be the biggest struggle. But a goal for me over time has become to try to be in prayer constantly, having a mental focus on bringing everything to God. A daily, hourly, minute-by-minute prayer. It is critically important.

Every time I pray, I feel better physically, mentally, and spiritually. Some people keep prayer logs. Some people pray with people. For me, I try to be in constant prayer. While I can fail miserably at that, I try to keep the concept of being prayerful at all times in my mind.

This verse from Proverbs 3:5–6 says it well: "Trust in the Lord with all your heart and lean not on your own understanding; in all your ways submit to him, and he will make your paths straight."

Following the leadership example of Christ is not something you only do on Sundays. It is something you constantly have to be aware of and focus on. Our lord Jesus Christ is our savior and went to the cross to save us from our sins. It is something of which I am constantly aware. Please remember as you read this book that as I acknowledge and understand Jesus Christ as the greatest leader, I am never intending to diminish the essential importance of Christ as our savior. I also want to acknowledge that in any of the Christ-centered faiths, or any faith journey, each of us must find our own path to that faith.

First, we start with Christ and his life on earth as our reference point and what we are called to do. From a Christian leadership standpoint, we look at Christ's example regarding how we are going to test situations in life.

The idea of participating in an organized church is hard for some people, but it should be a place where people support one another. It should be a place where people come together to work on the social issues of our time. Sometimes, we don't do that well in the Christian church, but it is something we constantly work on.

Many of the people I work with are people of deep faith, and some are religious but don't speak about it openly. The good news is that you can find fellowship at work as well as in the church.

No person can be strong all the time by themselves. You need people to help build you up. That said, close fellowship doesn't come naturally to me (and probably to many, and many others reading this). But you can learn to do a lot of things outside of your comfort zone. I have a thought that sometimes helps when it is time to *tie my top button*. This means when you are in a public setting as a Christian leader you are often going to work. When I go to corporate parties or big public events, I will often tell Barbara, "Well, I'm going to work. See you after the party." An event like that is often work, but taking that approach helps set expectations for why I am at the event.

Being intentional about participating in Bible study has had a positive impact for us. My wife grew up with perfect attendance at her Sunday school Bible classes and has pretty much had perfect attendance throughout her entire life in whatever she has done. That's not how I grew up!

For far too many people, prayer, Bible study, and Christian fellowship begin and end on Sunday. These are actions that need to happen every day, all day.

Every day, Jesus interacted with and helped people. He didn't interact with the religious leaders of the day; in fact, he took them on and exposed them for the sinners they were. Instead, his life was about helping the disabled, the downtrodden, and those in need, and he lived the life as a servant leader. In living this life, Christ went well beyond advocacy to lead by and through his actions.

Looking inside is the first step in leadership development. What comes from the heart is what defines you (Mark 7:20–23). We all make mistakes. We all mess up and lapse. But then you come back to and abide in Christ and his example of leadership, and that can help you in not getting caught up in the world.

You have to think internally about your perspective, your framework, your story, and how you are going to stay on the path. Start each day thinking about the Beatitudes and the Great Commandment, and let those values guide you in staying on the path. When people are focused on what is in it for them, that is dangerous. That's why it is important to get aligned first internally with your heart, soul, and mind.

When difficult decisions need to be made, or if you are in a crisis situation, self-reflection becomes even more important. You may feel the need to move quickly. But take a breath. Jesus would often retreat to the mountains before making critical decisions. He prayed. Look to the leadership example of Christ before making that critical decision, listen to others, be still for a moment, think about how your actions might impact others, and double-down on communication. And then act.

Once you have your internal focus fully developed, and as you continue to diligently prepare and practice a Christ-inspired leadership approach, you have to focus on two other aspects of leadership. As you think through how you are going to use the resources you have available in making an impact, you have to be patient and persistent as you are moving forward. Because it is a marathon.

Everyone needs a strong foundation that will hold solid during difficult times. Preparing for the narrow path, you need to walk slowly, carefully, and methodically, ensuring that each step is sure. Matthew 7:26–27 is one of those great Bible verses that can apply in many ways: "But everyone who hears these words of mine and does not put them into practice is like a foolish man who built his house on sand. The rain came down, the streams rose, and the winds blew and beat against that house, and it fell with a great crash." You should build your leadership approach, your life, and your family using Christ's example and teaching.

Use the Gospels to prioritize and organize. Christ focused on the Beatitudes and Sermon on the Mount. For me, the Beatitudes are like a looped tape that I want to run through the back of my mind all the time, an infinite reel running through my head at all times, influencing my values, how I lead, and the decisions I make every day at work and in life.

As important as preparation and patience is persistence. I think about the story of John Woolman, that American Quaker who during the mideighteenth century almost singlehandedly rid the Quaker Society of Friends of slaves. It took him decades to achieve his goal. He achieved that goal not by yelling loudly but through clear, gentle, persistent persuasion.

The social determinant story is an example of this concept. There is preparation from a Christian perspective. But at the beginning of launching this initiative and program, we were humble and didn't tell anyone, because we knew we had to build the story first. And more than ten years later, we are still working to help people understand the importance of addressing social and personal determinants of health. While we were moving forward rapidly in many ways, we needed to have patience as we extended the program. And we had to be persistent, because there were multiple times—and still are times—over the course of developing our social determinant program that we could have stopped, said, "This is enough. We've done good." But in our hearts, we knew there was so much more work to still be done. And we had to be persistent in working with our board members, our clinical leadership, and the community in understanding what we were doing and why.

Being a Christian leader at times is a lonely world. It is tough, and at times, the secular world doesn't help you. At times, you will feel like the odd person out. At times, you will feel like you really can't share what you feel or want to say. At times, it will cost you some friends or relationships. Be prepared.

The Beatitudes sound wonderful, and some in the corporate world might consider living the Beatitudes to be a soft goal. But to actually live the Beatitudes is extremely challenging, and if you dwell on it, it may seem almost impossible, if not impossible, to accomplish. When you read the Beatitudes and the Sermon on the Mount, you could look at yourself and say, "There is no sense to start, because there is no way I can accomplish all of this. No person could accomplish this every single day." When you start to dwell on these things, you can almost give up before you have even begun.

There are no shortcuts, no easy buttons to push as a Christian leader. Shaping you heart and mind to achieve the values of the Beatitudes is challenging. Servant leadership requires time and action as you are given opportunities and resources in life. And if you don't apply those gifts to helping others, then you have missed the mark.

It is a high bar. And as flawed humans who sin, it may seem impossible, but it is in the trying that counts.

The poet T. S. Eliot wrote in "Four Quartets," "For us, there is only the trying, the rest is not our business." There is so much wisdom in that statement. As we get older, we realize we are always limited, incomplete leaders. It is only through the grace of God we continue to move forward.

You can get great peace from prayer throughout your day. It can help you level set. Some pray in the shower in the morning, or in the car on the drive into work, or perhaps at set times during the day. Lately, I have been more intentional about praying on my knees. However or whenever you pray, it can have tremendous mental and physical benefits. It can help lower your blood pressure and help you to be more mindful. It's the ability to pray and ask for the guidance from the Holy Spirit. You pray for guidance for the day and being more open to listen. It gives you a sense of purpose and power.

As I go and pray on my knees, anxieties from my body drain away, and my perspective changes markedly. I wish I had been more faithful through my life doing this. It is cleansing.

Every time Christ faced a critical moment, he sought a solitary place where he could pray. It is a process I have followed increasingly as I have gotten older. These days, I pray every day to bless the organization. And understanding the tremendous resources our organization has available to make an impact in our communities, I pray that in leading the organization, we do the right thing. Prayer centers you and helps keep you on track.

2. Constantly Focus on Your Relationship with the Holy Spirit

In John 14:16, on the eve of his Crucifixion, Christ comforts the disciples and explains to them that he will send the Holy Spirit to help guide them. "If you love me, keep my commands. And I will ask the Father, and he will give you another advocate to help you and be with you forever – the Spirit of Truth." And in John 14:26, he notes that the Holy Spirit will teach the disciples all things and remind them of everything Christ has told them. A little later in this same passage, he talks about the Spirit of Truth who comes from the Father and will testify about Christ.

For some, the idea of the Holy Spirit may feel a little magical. And that was true for me earlier in my life. But as I get older, increasingly I pray and ask the Holy Spirit for guidance. And I listen. As I listen, receiving the guidance becomes more natural. The Holy Spirit provides a tremendous sense of peace and calm. You feel you are not alone, that you have a powerful ally. Your words, your decisions, and your actions are buoyed by the Holy Spirit. We are all incomplete beings. As we open our heart during prayer, the Holy Spirit becomes a moral compass, directing us to do the right thing and guarding us against self-focused longings to get what we want and perhaps selfishly think we are deserved and owed—what we might consider to be the trappings of leadership. We are blessed to have a Spirit of Truth advocating for us all.

The importance and value of the Holy Spirit is summarized well in 1 Corinthians 2:10–12: "The Spirit searches all things, even the deep things of God. For who knows a person's thoughts except their own spirit within them? In the same way no one knows the thoughts of God except the Spirit of God. What we have received is not the spirit of the world, but the Spirit who is from God, so that we may understand what God has freely given us."

And as we live in accordance with Holy Spirit, we will come to receive the fruit of the Holy Spirit: love, joy, peace, patience, kindness, goodness, faithfulness, gentleness, and self-control.

I share more about my faith now than ever before. As I have taken on more responsibility and had more opportunities, I understand that we must be accountable for making the most impact possible based on our resources and our faith. I have to live out my life as best I can with a transcending purpose—one that will have impact on people's lives. And that is what I am going to be held accountable for. As part of that, we have to have an honest conversation with ourselves and think of things from the perspective of others.

3. The Greatest Leadership Example Is Right in Front of You—Jesus Christ

Christ was the ultimate servant leader, summed up so well in Matthew 20:26–27: "Whoever wants to be first must be your slave …" One of the last things Christ did was to wash the feet of his disciples, and then he told them to go and wash the feet of others. It was an ultimate example of last being first and the first being last. There are many contemporary authors and leadership experts in the secular world who write about the concept of servant leadership. We will talk about them later in the chapter on servant leadership, but Christ was perhaps the original example of this principle.

When you look at Christ's life, he had a clear mission and values. God's mission for Christ was to save all of us from our sins. His mission was the Great Commission, to make fishers of men who would spread the good word and make disciples of nations. The values were embodied by the Beatitudes and the lessons from the Sermon on the Mount. To some, the Beatitudes (e.g., blessed are the poor in spirit, the meek, the merciful, the peacemakers) may seem like soft values, but to actually live them requires tremendous discipline and a life's commitment to follow that narrow path. As a Christian leader, you can do that in ways that are nuanced and advocate for Christ and his leadership style through your actions.

The point is that all major leadership principles have the greatest leadership example already in Christ. He was the ultimate servant leader. Later in the book, we are going to talk about leading change and compare the work of contemporary leadership experts and authors to the leadership example of Christ, who led the most radical change in history. When you think of time management, no one beats Christ, who changed the world in three years. What we will highlight is that these great leadership and management ideas are perfectly illustrated by way Christ lived, taught, and led.

Focusing on purpose, mission, values, and culture are critical contemporary leadership areas of focus. Christ is a timelessly contemporary example of having purpose, a mission, and values and establishing a culture of change.

Christ was a true example of respecting and not judging others. That is not to say that Christ didn't judge; he did at times, but he loved us in spite of our sins and flaws. He valued women during a time where they weren't valued. He cared for the lepers, the disabled, those with mental and physical issues. He cared for the sinners of the day, those rejected by society, those with little education.

Later in the book, we are going to talk about making an impact relative to your talents, your resources, and your faith, a concept that was identified (with a few tweaks by me) by Jim Collins in his brilliant book, *Good to Great and the Social Sectors.* Christ challenged us all to do just that.

I have often thought that many of our leadership experts owe the church and Christ a royalty since they in many ways are copying his work and creating new secular metaphors to express his leadership example. Just think about it: concepts like emotional intelligence, leading change, communication via stories, servant leadership, recognizing that we are all incomplete leaders,* and the need for mission, vision, and values. Christ exemplified all these things during his brief ministry.

Many people have said Christ was a leader, but that wasn't his primary purpose. Christ came to save us from our sins. That mission doesn't minimize the fact that he was also an incredible leader—the greatest of all time. Great leaders are often great teachers and vice versa. Some may call him the great teacher but not the greatest leader. But truly, these are often synonymous!

4. Test and Consider What the Secular World Offers for Consideration

The secular world has many wonderful things to offer. It is important that as you search and ask questions, you should test what the secular world has to offer. In the chapter on life purpose, we will focus on conversations I have had with a behavioral scientist and how the outcome of finding a transcending purpose can be similar for both the scientist and the Christian. Both may reach the outcome from entirely different perspectives—and that's okay.

Earlier in this chapter, I mentioned the Bible study group where we focused on popular leadership books of the time and began to test them against scripture. What came as an initial shock quickly became almost routine as we matched the insights made by these researchers and authors with similar principles that were clearly laid out in scripture. While the secular world provides many opportunities for growth, the test for Christians is to test these ideas against scripture and the example of Christ. The two can coexist.

Instead of just reacting to new secular leadership article or book of the day, consider a Christian framework, based on Christ's leadership example. Otherwise, you will pull from nothing but secular sources. As we have seen throughout the book, a lot of secular leadership thinking and writing is based on the leadership example of Christ, whether acknowledged or not.

We have tried to take the secular and apply it to Christianity, instead of just looking at the leadership from the examples of Christ. What happens from that is that there will be a natural tension there. The sexiness of the secular, the YouTube video of the day, these hip management consultants, and the new buzzword of the day—that is often what you see and hear at work. So there will always be a natural tension in that environment. And that can lead to Christianized leadership.

The challenge is to flip that. First, try taking the leadership examples of Christ and apply those in the secular world. Consider the concept of *Emotional Intelligence*, Daniel Goldman's book. The first time I read the book, I thought it was brilliant (still do actually), but then I looked back at the Gospels and compared scripture to what Goldman had written and thought, *Well, it's all there. Why didn't I see that before?* So instead of reading the current leadership books, start with the Gospels.

What would be really interesting would be to compile all the various best-selling leadership books over the years and see if you could find examples of key management/leadership principles that aren't already illustrated in the Gospels. I am guessing it might be hard to find new principles that aren't in some way already in the Gospels unless they come from a purely secular foundation.

When considering secular and Christian leadership, there will be tension from living your life consistently from Sunday to the workplace. I worked for a person who, when I initially interviewed with him, seemed the ideal in Christian leadership. But after working for him, I found him to be the opposite, a complete narcissist who took advantage of people for his own gain.

As you live a purposeful leadership life, you have to tighten up your spine and have your own ideas. Everyone's story is different. Having your story, your path, and an understanding of what you believe Christ is calling you to do is incredibly important. I had a particular foundation growing up in Iowa. Over the years, I have taken a broad-based view of life, but I always have that foundation of Christ and the Holy Spirit to fall back on, and that gives me great strength as a leader.

5. Strive to Live a Life Marked by Character and Integrity

Most of us are wired to be good, and we strive to lead good lives and to do good things. But it is just too easy to say that only with words.

Jesus offers us the example of how a Christian leader should lead a life marked by character and integrity; it is not nearly as important to talk about his leadership example as it is to actually be that example, essentially advocating through action. It reminds me of the phrase "What would Jesus do?" often seen as the acronym WWJD, which was inspired by a book written in the late 1800s with the title *In His Steps: What Would Jesus Do?* by Reverend Charles Sheldon. The phrase became popular again for Christians in the 1990s as a call to emulate the love of Jesus. And it also is the great principle underlying the leadership example of Christ.

That said, some began to take that phrase as a marketing tool. For example, in the early 2000s, there was an advertising campaign that took the phrase out of context to say, "What would Jesus drive?"

I try to think not about what Jesus would have done but what he actually did do. I find myself reading and rereading the Gospels of Mark, Matthew, Luke, and John, and in particular the Sermon on the Mount and the Beatitudes, because they are retellings of what Christ did during his three-year ministry.

I try to constantly keep in the forefront and meditate on both Christ's leadership example and how my thoughts and actions impact others. Think about the words we say, the things we do, the social media content we post. Are we a positive influence or negative influence? Are we trying to do the best we can?

Compassion oftentimes creates action. In the Gospels, Christ's displays of compassion were oftentimes immediately followed by action, whether it was a miracle, a sign, or some other deed. Whether people are trapped in generational poverty, losing their job, or are experiencing prejudice or systemic racism and violence, you have to have compassion and use your resources to make a difference. That is what we are called to do. That is what we are going to be held accountable for.

Christ was motivated to act as a result of his compassion for people, in saving people, healing people, and bringing them to God. He was compassionate to women and children, to those who were physically challenged, disabled, and mentally ill, and to those most in need. And he used that compassion to win over people. Just as in everyday life today, people see people working to help others, and normally people respond to that. In the same way, as Christ helped people, the masses of people responded to him.

You advocate with your actions, not just with words. In addressing the social determinants of health, we took action to start addressing obesity and then hunger insecurity in a quiet, humble fashion. As we had successes, momentum and advocacy for what we were doing took off, followed by increased and expanding action over the last decade.

Leading by Christ's leadership example doesn't mean you have to be overt about it. Christ was very careful. At times when he performed miracles, he would tell onlookers to not tell anyone else about them. Then there were times, with the money changers for example, where he took strong action. He met people where they were, and his leadership style changed depending on who he was with and the environment he was in. But you don't have to be militant in your faith every day, all day to be a Christian leader. The quote from St. Francis is so appropriate: "Go forth and spread the Gospel by every means possible. If necessary, use words."

I have always been more subtle in finding opportunities to express my faith. It may be my Dutch reformation upbringing, but I have never worn my religion on my sleeve, focusing more on actions rather than overtly talking about my faith. But over the years, particularly in the last 11 years as a president and CEO, I have been more comfortable sharing that my faith has a definite impact on my decision-making.

The work that our organization has implemented over the last decade related to health inequity and social determinants has been clearly motivated by my faith. Our programs related to food insecurity, financial security, housing, economic development, community development, and others all are solidly rooted in the principles of servant leadership. These are actions that a health care organization should be taking. While our organization is not a faith-based organization, these actions are clearly the right thing to do for the communities and people we serve. It is a place where the secular world and my faith interact successfully. But we take these actions with humility.

Over the centuries, scholars have used different terms to describe leaders who falsely represent Christianity. In this book, we used the terms wide-path leaders and wide-path organizations. For wide-path leaders, it is the "Gospel according to me." They see themselves as the personal gatekeepers of God's law, with the purpose of maintaining their own authority, and they see themselves as becoming of greater importance, minimizing Christ. Whether intentional or not, the popularization of non-Christian leadership is an incredible disservice and a mistake for leadership. Wide-path organizations are more concerned about ensuring their own existence than the cross. They are corporatized and mainly focused on numbers as ways to measure success rather than on the meaning of Christ's message. We need to help these leaders change, and if they don't, avoid these leaders and organizations.

In Matthew 23:3–30, there are a series of "Woe to you" statements that nicely capture the negative attributes of the Pharisees. Among the key points are: they say one thing but do another; they use a double standard to justify their actions; they may look nice on the outside but are corrupt on the inside; they seem to be spiritually alive but on the inside are withered; they put a heavy burden on others but none on themselves; and they are self-righteous. These are the same questions we need to be asking as Christian leaders.

In Matthew 5:17, Christ declares to his disciples that he wasn't on earth to abolish the law but to fulfill it. Seems like a pretty clear statement. But he then proceeds to refine rules and extend boundaries. He adds the Beatitudes and the Great Commandment. He takes rules and then declares the antithesis of that rule, saying, "You may have heard it said, but I say to you ..." He works on the Sabbath, which at that time was not allowed and was scorned by the Pharisees. These seeming inconsistencies become more understandable when you consider that Christ was rigorously upholding God's laws but was willing to make changes and correct human-made rules. The Pharisees had added tons of rules with the sole purpose of solidifying their power and authority, and Christ called them out on it. In addition, the Beatitudes and Great Commandment totally flipped what was the reality of the day, so he extended boundaries. We are challenged to do the same thing in our own way.

Jesus's narrow path was focused on the poor in spirit, the mourners, the meek, the merciful, the pure at heart, and the peacemakers. In many ways, in this "me too" world we live in today, following this path is as new today as it was during Christ's time. Because it requires discipline and strength to follow this path.

As he defined reality in this way, Christ forced choices. In Luke 12:51–52, Jesus says, "Do you think I came to bring peace on earth? No ..." When you create urgency, you create some divisions. That may seem a little harsh at times, but that is exactly what it is about. So sometimes we are forced to choose, and not choosing is a choice. As leaders, that is sometimes what we must do—we must force a choice.

Christ wasn't a Democrat, he wasn't a Republican, he wasn't a liberal or a conservative, and he wasn't an independent. For Christians, it cannot be either/or. It is more like yes/and. Christian values cut across all parties. Christ tended to those in need, not to those in positions of power.

We are becoming a nation even more isolated inside our own belief silos. We hear what we want to hear and ignore other points of view and become incredibly intolerant of one another. It is not ours to judge or to be an avenger. To get to yes/and, we need to become more accepting of all points of view.

How Do You Measure Success?

Clayton Christensen, a very religious person, wrote a great article that was published in 2010 in *Harvard Business Review* (and he also wrote a book) about how you measure your life.[2] He was a devout Mormon. And he recognized that the most powerful motivator isn't money; it is the need to learn, grow, and contribute in meaningful ways. He asked about how we are going to mark success. How are you going to measure your life? Is it how much money you make, how you succeeded at work, how many rounds of golf you played after you retired, or is it something beyond that? When I look back on what we have accomplished relative to the social determinants of life, that will be one way that I will measure my life.

As a member of the board of an art museum, I learned about docents, volunteers who offer tours for children and adults to help ensure they have a rewarding experience at the museum, and they help find ways to connect art to the lives of people. They spend countless hours and years learning about art and art history as they learn to be docents. The docents have to have the mental capacity and ability to tell stories and build narratives that help people understand and appreciate art, impacting people's lives in very real ways. Their blessing is their love of art, and what they are doing is helping others have great experiences at a museum, which hopefully helps lead people to have a lifelong relationship with art. That can impact people's lives in very real ways. These are volunteers who are often very successful people in life, and they take that blessing and give back to the community in very real and vibrant ways.

You begin to think about using your talents and how you can you use your skill set to help others. We all have blessings, but it is what we do with the blessing that counts.

The key measurement in business is no longer just the ability to make money for its shareholders. That doesn't mean you have to have tons of money to make an impact. You can impact without any money or resources.

I have been blessed to work at organizations that have resources that we can use to benefit not only the community but our employees. At the end of 2020 and as COVID dragged on, we decided to give all employees a $750 bonus. For many people, that really helped make a difference in their lives. And we also raised our minimum wage. One lady sent me a nice email after we sent out the bonus. She was involved in a Big Brother / Big Sister program, and she used her bonus to help a grandmother who was helping many other kids. This is one of our service workers who is now helping out another grandmother. It was inspirational that this service worker was doing what she could with the resources available to her. It was powerful.

There are many ways to measure success. As Christian leaders, our approach to work and life has to be with the heart of a servant, staying humble and each day striving to live the example of Christ through the Beatitudes and Great Commandment, and we need to measure our accomplishments against those standards.

Taking the Narrow Path to an Expansive Perspective

Throughout this book, one of the main things we have been working toward is a definition of the phrase *narrow path*. Certainly, the narrow path can be immediately applied to the doctrinal principles of TULIP. We are all flawed humans, with all too human failings. It is easy to be influenced to take a wide path of sin.

But taking the narrow path does not mean narrow-mindedness. Taking the narrow path requires more. It is a disciplined focus on living the Beatitudes and the principles expressed in the Sermon on the Mount, which are the opposite of narrow-mindedness. It is about not falling into the trap of Christianized leadership and organizations saying one thing but, through their actions, clearly taking a wide path that is about them and not the least of these. That commitment takes discipline, patience, and persistence. It requires you to apply your faith, your blessing, and the resources at your disposal and to make a real and lasting impact in your community—every day. To do that, you must have an expansive vision and action.

Throughout my career, I have tended to compartmentalize my faith life from my work life. In the introduction of this book, I talked about two presentations I was working on at the same time, one related to work, one related to my faith. I had a stack of folders for my work presentation and another stack for my religious presentation. And then they tumbled together. And it just hit me how those two presentations and those two separate worlds needed to be combined, because we are better off when we integrate secular and sacred.

I think most Christians often compartmentalize life, and they feel, *There is my church life, and there is my work life, and there is my home life.* Most can't or won't bridge the gap. Sometimes, either subtly or not so subtly, we have led people to compartmentalize because we haven't given them a way to integrate it. As Christian leaders, we should help one another integrate the sacred and the secular.

There was the pastor who told me I had to quit my job because it was interfering with my church work. I couldn't quit my job. I had three children. We need to overcome that insensitivity and find positive ways to integrate the two worlds. As we have seen throughout this book, combining the secular and the sacred can lead to spectacular innovation and improve health and well-being for individuals and communities.

If all you are doing is compartmentalizing your life to a few small people who love you, that probably won't do much good, because they are going to love you anyway. But when you are out in the world and growing, and they can see you minister to your faith, you get outside of yourself, and the world is a better place. If you believe a certain thing, no matter how much contrary information you receive, you will still tend to not give up your belief. The only way to overcome that is to bombard yourself with information and totally immerse yourself in the world of ideas, and you will find great opportunities to do the kinds of things Christians should do.

So you have this foundation in life and have prepared yourself to be on this narrow path. At the same time, with the guidance of the Holy Spirit, you open yourself up to new information and new vistas. By taking the narrow path while maintaining a broad perspective, you will navigate your life narrative in a very different way.

We think of being with Christ, but we compartmentalize it outside of leadership. As we go to work each day, whether from a home office or a location elsewhere, we need to act like him, be like him, and lead like him. Through his example as the greatest leader who ever lived, Jesus Christ showed us how to lead, how to have compassion, how to live with grace and humility. It is about trying to walk a narrow path, approaching life with an expansive perspective, led by Jesus Christ and the Holy Spirit, and emulating Christ's leadership example. Nothing could be more rewarding.

"As We Rise Each Day"

As we rise each day,
We strive
Faithfully
To follow your lead.

Taking the narrow path
Far from the wide walk
Of the world.

Step by step,
We are bolstered
By your majesty.

A path ordained
By you.

We step into the glory
Of your creation.
We marvel at your holiness,
Jesus's life, death, and resurrection.

Your path
Is a place of refuge;
Your Word
Lights our path
Brilliantly;
Your grace
Covers our doubts,
Our fears,
And our loneliness.

We step forward
In all humility,
At the urging
Of the Holy Spirit,
With faith
And the example of Christ
To make our path
Straight and true.

RD Oostra
June 2022

APPENDIX

Bible Verses to Consider as a Christ-Inspired Leader

What follows are some essential Bible verses I used in the book (and a few additional verses not included) that have been useful to me over the years as I have thought about Jesus Christ and his leadership example, along with brief commentary about why the verses were important to me. These Bible verses generally follow the narrative of this book but not completely so. In a few cases where there are extended verses, to save space, I cite the verses but do not provide the text.

At the end of this appendix are several blank pages where you can add your own favorite Bible verses as you continue your Christ-inspired journey along the narrow path to expansive perspective.

On Miracles

> "Because you have seen me, you have believed; blessed are those who have not seen and yet have believed." (John 20:29)

Christ says this to Thomas at the moment he is doubting the miracle of the resurrection. Christ blesses those who did not have the opportunity to see the resurrection and still believed. For Christ, it was actually at least as important that those who didn't see the miracle became believers. They were perhaps the more blessed because they didn't need to see the miracle to believe.

Jesus performed many other signs in the presence of his disciples, which are not recorded in this book. But these are written that you may believe that Jesus is the Messiah, the Son of God, and that by believing you may have life in his name. (John 20:30–31)

John replaces the word *miracles* with the word *signs* throughout his Gospel. And like the miracles, these signs result in outcomes that lead people to true faith. So the concept of signs and miracles can be synonymous. Christ did say he would perform miracles as signs so that people would believe. He also said blessed were those who believe who didn't see these miracles. The signs pointed people to God. I embrace the science and look at it through a Christian lens, and the combined perspective has helped make me a better leader.

On the Truth

To the Jews who had believed him, Jesus said, "If you hold to my teaching, you are really my disciples. Then you will know the truth, and the truth will set you free." (John 8:31–32)

Many people know the widely quoted section of this verse that says, "The truth will set you free."

But fewer people are as familiar with the entire verse, which says, "To the Jews who had believed him, Jesus said, 'If you hold to my teaching, you are really my disciples. Then you will know the truth, and the truth will set you free.'" Truth comes from Christ's teaching and leadership example, and that is what we need to hold on to.

On Humility

"I tell you that this man, rather than the other, went home justified before God. For all those who exalt themselves will be humbled, and those who humble themselves will be exalted." (Luke 18:14)

Wide-path leaders tend to be self-righteous, which Jesus vividly illustrates in the parable of the Pharisee and the tax collector. One exemplifies the Roman culture, while the other represents a more Christian culture. As the two go to the temple to pray, the Pharisee represents the empire, while the tax collector resists Roman occupation and law. One embraces the culture; the other rejects it. As they pray, the Pharisee is prideful; the tax collector pleads for mercy. Their words reveal their hearts.

On What's Important

> "Do not work for food that spoils, but for food that endures to eternal life." (John 6:27)

After Jesus feeds the five thousand, he goes to the mountain in retreat, and when he returns, he finds the disciples looking for him. Christ tells the disciples that they were looking for him not because of the signs he performed in feeding the five thousand but because of the food they ate. We get enticed, reinforced, and encouraged by the secular world to think of ourselves, but Christ would encourage us to do the opposite.

On Servant Leadership

> Blessed are the poor in spirit,
> for theirs is the Kingdom of Heaven.
> Blessed are those who mourn,
> for they will be comforted.
> Blessed are the meek,
> for they will inherit the Earth.
> Blessed are those who hunger and thirst for righteousness,
> for they will be filled.
> Blessed are the merciful,
> for they will be shown mercy.
> Blessed are the pure in heart,
> for they will see God.
> Blessed are the peacemakers,

for they will be called children of God.

Blessed are those who are persecuted because of righteousness,

for theirs is the Kingdom of Heaven. (Matthew 5:3–12)

Whether you are Protestant, a Catholic, another religion, or a person who is not sure what they believe, considering these Beatitudes provides you a structure and a point of view. You look at faith in all kinds of ways and how we are going to apply it. Some might consider the Beatitudes as soft values. In fact, they help define a very certain, very narrow path that requires great discipline to achieve.

"Anyone who wants to be first must be the very last, and the servant of all." (Mark 9:35)

"So the last will be first, and the first will be last." (Matthew 20:16)

"But you are not to be like that. Instead, the greatest among you should be like the youngest, and the one who rules like the one who serves." (Luke 22:26)

The motivation to lead changes completely when you begin to think about the leadership example of Christ as servant leader. The motivation is not to be in charge. The motivation is to serve.

"Truly I tell you, whatever you did for one of the least of these brothers and sisters of mine, you did for me."

"Truly I tell you, whatever you did not do for one of the least of these, you did not do for me." (Matthew 25:40, 45)

The parable about the sheep and the goat is more than about how a shepherd separates the sheep from the goats. It is about servant leadership.

"My command is this: Love each other as I have loved you."

"Love your neighbor as yourself." (John 15:12, Mark 12:31, Matthew 22:39, Luke 10:27)

How are we supposed to consider the second half of the Great Commandment? Mark, Matthew, and Luke use the word *neighbor*, where John does not. How do you define neighbor? When you look at the historic context, a neighbor might have been defined literally as the person next to you or the country next to you. But as Christ refined scripture, he added a broader context to suggest that a neighbor can mean literally anyone.

On the Antivalues

The "Woe to you" verses (Matthew 23:13–16, 23, 25, 27).

There are eight woes of the Pharisees found in these verses. The Gospels not only suggest the kind of values we should strive for through the Beatitudes and the Great Commandment; they have kind of antivalues or behaviors/actions we should be careful about. The woes largely criticize the Pharisees for their hypocrisy and perjury and illustrate moral and ethical concepts. The Pharisees taught about God but did not love Him. They taught law but did not practice justice, mercy, or faithfulness to God. Outwardly, they appeared clean, but they were tarnished internally. They pretended to be righteous but were the opposite. This is the essence of a wide-path leader.

On Judging

> "Do not judge, or you too will be judged. For in the same way
> you judge others, you will be judged, and with the measure
> you use, it will be measured to you." (Matthew 7:1–2)

Sometimes people make strong, harsh judgments about people and their lives, yet we try to decide which sins are more important than others. The Bible doesn't prioritize sins. We do that. So how can you judge others? I was brought up believing certain actions were sinful, but as you mature as a Christian, you realize that so much of what we do is sinful; so how do you judge certain sins and ignore others? The older I get, the less (hopefully) I judge others. Don't presume you know what is in someone's head. What you need to do is try to understand the other person's story. It is how you treat people and give them the benefit of the doubt until you understand their story.

He went on: "What comes out of a person is what defiles them. For it is from within, out of a person's heart, that evil thoughts come—sexual immorality, theft, murder, adultery, greed, malice, deceit, lewdness, envy, slander, arrogance and folly. All these evils come from inside and defile a person." (Mark 7:20–23)

An initial step in leadership development is to look inside first, because that is where it all starts. Christ talks about how what comes out of a person's heart is what defines and defiles them. That relates to what you put into your body spiritually as well as physically, abiding in Christ, who you hang with, what you focus on every day. We all make mistakes. We all mess up and lapse. But then you come back to and abide in Christ, making sure from the inside out you are thinking and living the Christian life, not getting caught up in the world, and then being really focused on the conviction to be a leader in Christ's image. That conviction includes not just your beliefs but the values you use, the commitments you make, and the motivation you have in dealing with the challenges of each day.

A good man brings good things out of the good stored up in his heart, and an evil man brings evil things out of the evil stored up in his heart. The mouth speaks what the heart is full of. (Luke 6:45)

Words matter. Who we are inside will be revealed by our actions at some point. As a Christian leader, the degree to which we walk closely with Jesus, the more our words will be evidence that we follow him and that we are true to our actions. The Holy Spirit will help us in being thoughtful, gracious, and true. For any leader, we know that who we are inside will ultimately be known through our words and actions.

"But everyone who hears these words of mine and does not put them into practice is like a foolish man who built his house on sand. The rain came down, the streams rose, and the winds blew and beat against that house, and it fell with a great crash." (Matthew 7:26–27)

Having a strong foundation in life is critical. And it is not just listening but putting words in action. When you begin to think about the challenges in life and what you should rely on, everyone needs a strong foundation that will hold sold during those difficult times. Preparing for the narrow path, you need to walk slowly, carefully, and methodically, ensuring that when you take a step forward, it is a sure step. We want to make sure those fundamental principles we step on are solid as rock. And that foundation is Christ.

On Having Faith

He said to his disciples, "Why are you so afraid? Do you still have no faith?" (Mark 4:40)

The twelve disciples Jesus picked had many failings; they were unprepared, they lacked perspective and vision, they often drew wrong conclusions, and they even rejected Christ. There were times when they clearly just didn't get the parables. They had their own desires and reasons for following Christ. They were overconfident and had petty squabbles over rank and who was the greatest among them. At other times, they lacked confidence. When there was the storm at sea, even though Peter, Andrew, James, and John were experienced fishermen, they were afraid of being shipwrecked. Jesus calmed the waters and had to build their confidence, telling them to have faith.

He said to his disciples, "Why are you so afraid? Do you still have no faith?" (John 14:1)

While Christ could be hard on his disciples as he developed them, he also spent time comforting them and reassuring them. As a leader, you create a sense of urgency, and you challenge people, but there is a fine line between challenging people and acknowledging them, telling them they are doing a great job and to keep it up.

On Heading toward Trouble

See John 11:1–10.

Jesus tells the disciples that they are returning to Judea, a place the disciples remind Jesus where there were those who tried to stone him. And yet Jesus wants to return to that environment. That is what true leaders do; they are willing to walk where others might not go, which is part of the hard work of being a disciple. You don't want to walk away from trouble; walk in. That is what Christ did.

On Extending Grace

> On the evening of that first day of the week, when the disciples were together, with the doors locked for fear of the Jewish leaders, Jesus came and stood among them and said, "Peace be with you!" (John 20:19)

The first thing Christ said to the disciples at the moment he was reunited with them following the resurrection was "Peace be with you." He extended his grace. He always extended grace. Think about the moments in your life when someone has extended grace to you, and those times when you have had opportunities to extend grace. You can do this when you frame up your mind and your attitude so that in tough situations, you can be in the right position mentally to react with grace. We are incomplete, and Christ calls on us all to extend grace to everyone. In the same way that we extend grace to others, it is a gift for us as well, because doing so provides internal peace, confidence, and assurance to us through the Holy Spirit as we go about our daily lives.

On Being Childlike

> And he said: 'Truly I tell you, unless you turn and become like children, you will never enter the kingdom of heaven." (Matthew 18:3)

This verse is an indicator of how Christ supported and accepted children, but it is also a key to many other things like acceptance, innocence, and innovation. To think like a child and take that leap of imagination needed, either to be born again or in finding new ways of doing things, is a critical characteristic of a leader.

On Prayer

> Do not be anxious about anything, but in every situation, by prayer and petition, with thanksgiving, present your requests to God. And the peace of God, which transcends all understanding, will guard your hearts and your minds in Christ Jesus. (Philippians 4:6–7)

Prayer is one of the key ways I am able to achieve perspective. Today, my prayer life is better than it has been at any time in my life. That said, while it is better, I still need to improve. To sum the benefits up nicely, we all need the peace of God.

See Matthew 6:5–15.

Jesus and the disciples give us guidance not only on the need to pray but on how to pray. It is important to be humble and private in prayer. As in, when you pray, go to a private space; and when you pray, don't be a hypocrite and pray in the public. Don't babble on, because it is not about the length of the prayer but the quality of the prayer. Be respectful. It is all about what is motivating you to pray. Ultimately, it is about having a prayerful relationship with Christ.

On the Holy Spirit

> These are the things God has revealed to us by his Spirit. The Spirit searches all things, even the deep things of God. For who knows a person's thoughts except their own spirit within them? In the same way no one knows the thoughts of God except the Spirit of God. What we have received is not the spirit of the world, but the Spirit who is from God, so that we may understand what God has freely given us. (1 Corinthians 2:10–12)

My message and my preaching were not with wise and persuasive words, but with a demonstration of the Spirit's power, so that your faith might not rest on human wisdom, but on God's power. (1 Corinthians 2:4–5)

"But very truly I tell you, it is for your good that I am going away. Unless I go away, the Advocate will not come to you; but if I go, I will send him to you." (John 16:7)

"But the Advocate, the Holy Spirit, whom the Father will send in my name, will teach you all things and will remind you of everything I have said to you." (John 14:26)

But the fruit of the Spirit is love, joy, peace, forbearance, kindness, goodness, faithfulness, gentleness and self-control. Against such things there is no law. (Galatians 5:22–23)

Your words, your decisions, how you process decisions all benefit from the moral compass of the Holy Spirit. When you think about that every day and you pray it, open yourself, and pray to the Holy Spirit for guidance, it starts to impact your mind and softens your heart in a positive way.

Jesus provided practical advice. He showed the example of prayer, the example of compassion to all people, and how to relate to people who weren't in authority, and he gave them tools and the power of the Holy Spirit, which would provide guidance and comfort throughout their lives.

It is through our faith and the guidance of the Holy Spirit that we can find truth and avoid faulty rationalization. The need to look to the Holy Spirit for guidance is spelled out in this Bible verse. For me, understanding and appreciation of the Holy Spirit is greater today than ever in my life.

On Trust

Trust in the Lord with all your heart and lean not on your own understanding; in all your ways submit to him, and he will make your paths straight. (Proverbs 3:5–6)

Following the leadership example of Christ is not something you do only on Sundays. It is something you constantly have to be aware of and focus on. Our Lord Jesus Christ is our savior and went to the cross to save us from our sins. It is something of which I am constantly aware. Every time I pray, I feel better physically, mentally, and spiritually. Some people keep prayer logs. Some people pray with people. For me, I try to be in constant prayer. While I can fail miserably at that, I try to keep the concept of being prayerful at all times in my mind.

On Becoming Complete

> "Until now you have not asked for anything in my name.
> Ask and you will receive, and your joy will be complete."
> (John 16:24)

We are all incomplete leaders; we are all flawed; we are all imperfect; we are all sinful. It is Christ who completes us: The complete leader is the one who follows the Beatitudes, is humble, is constantly seeking to grow, pays attention to others, and follows the principles of Christ's leadership. When we are solidly following Christ's leadership and applying that leadership approach to our lives, we are the most complete leader we can be. We become more complete leaders, we become more empathetic, and we become better listeners. It becomes who we are.

Bible Verses Related to Thinking about Mission and Values

God's Mission for Christ

- "To save us from our sins" (John 3:17).

Christ's Mission for Us

- "To go and make disciples of all nations, baptizing them in the name of the Father, and of the Son, and of the Holy Spirit, and teaching them to obey everything I have commanded you" (Matthew 28:16–20) (the Great Commission).

Christ's Values

- "Love the Lord your God with your heart, soul, and mind" (Matthew 22:35–39) (the Great Commandment).
- "Love your neighbor as yourself" (Matthew 22:35–39) (the Great Commandment).
- "Live the Beatitudes" (Matthew 5:3–12).

The Antivalues

- The woes of the Pharisees (Matthew 23, verses 13–16, 23, 25, 27, and 29).

Bible Verses Related to Leading Change

To help illustrate the connection between Christ's leadership style and contemporary experts who have created models for leading change, what follows is a little bit of a deep dive into a contemporary secular concept in leading change compared to Christ's leadership example. Throughout this chapter, we will provide each step in John Kotter's process and then show how Christ lived the concept thousands of years ago. In addition, I will offer a few examples of how we implement these processes for change at my organization. You can decide if the style reflects Christ's leadership approach or Kotter's eight-step process.

Jesus's Change Process	Kotter's Eight-Stage Process	Relevant Bible Verse(s)
Took on status quo; identified failed leadership; reinterpreted and extended the Torah (while still seeking to fulfill the Torah); acted in counterintuitive ways; worked on Sabbath; reshaped the exercise of piety; almsgiving, prayer, fasting	Establishing a sense of urgency	Luke 10:3–4, 10:9 Mark 11:15–18 Matthew 5:17–40 Luke 20:27–40 (interpretation of burning bush story) Matthew 6:1–18 Mark 11:27–33
Identified and brought in the disciples and apostles; built coalition among those who were in need; extended and reinterpreted the Torah; established and sent out the seventy-two	Creating a guiding coalition	Luke 6:12–49 Luke 10
Identified mission and values; identified wanted behaviors (the Great Commandment; the Beatitudes); identified unwanted behaviors (the woes); articulated a vision of being fishers of men, making disciples of all the nations	Developing a vision and strategy	Mission: Matthew 6:33; Vision: Matthew 28:16–20 Values: Matthew 22:3–39; 10–12; 15–17; 3–12; 6:19–?) Mark 12:29–34 Luke 6:27–36

Jesus's Change Process	Kotter's Eight-Stage Process	Relevant Bible Verse(s)
Communication through disciples/ apostles sending out messengers; Gospels; sermons; letters; parables; modeled change; asking questions; defining reality; providing instructions	Communicating the change vision	Matthew 1:1–42 Matthew 28:18–20 Luke 9:52
Sent disciples out and empowered them to achieve the Great Commission; the power of prayer	Empowering broad-based action	Matthew 10 Luke 10–16 Mark 6:7–13
Performed miracles	Generating short-term wins	Mark 1:29–34, 40–42
Repeatedly in Acts, the ongoing success of the church's mission is stressed in summaries that mark its progress: Christians succeed not only in being faithful disciples themselves but also in "turning the world upside down" in having a transforming effect on society. Numerous stories present the church as triumphant over all forms of evil, wiping out poverty, healing diseases.	Consolidation gains and producing more change	Acts: 1:14; 2:41; 4:4; 5:14; 6:7; 9:31; 11:21, 24; 12:24; 14:1; 16:5; 19:20; 28:30–31 Acts 17:6 Acts 4:32–37 Acts 5:12–16 Luke 10:17–18
Disciples/apostles get out the word; creation of the New Testament, including the four Gospels; prioritizing actions	Anchoring new approaches in the culture	Matthew 6
Took on status quo; identified failed leadership; reinterpreted and extended the Torah (while still seeking to fulfill the Torah); acted in counterintuitive ways; worked on Sabbath; reshaped the exercise of piety; almsgiving, prayer, fasting	Establishing a sense of urgency	Luke 10:3–4, 10:9 Mark 11:15–18 Matthew 5:17–40 Exodus 3 v Luke 20:27–40 (interpretation of burning bush story) Matthew 6:1–18 Mark 11:27–33

Jesus's Change Process	Kotter's Eight-Stage Process	Relevant Bible Verse(s)
Identified and brought in the disciples and apostles; built coalition among those who were in need; extended and reinterpreted the Torah; established and sent out the seventy-two	Creating a guiding coalition	Luke 6:12–49 Luke 10
Identified mission and values; identified wanted behaviors (the Great Commandment; the Beatitudes); identified unwanted behaviors (the woes); articulated a vision of being fishers of men, making disciples of all the nations	Developing a vision and strategy	Mission: Matthew 6:33; Vision: Matthew 28:16–20 Values: Matthew 22:3–39; 10–12; 15–17; 3–12; 6:19–?) Mark 12:29–34 Luke 6:27–36
Communication through disciples/ apostles sending out messengers; Gospels; sermons; letters; parables; modeled change; asking questions; defining reality; providing instructions	Communicating the change vision	Matthew 1:1–42 Matthew 28:18–20 Luke 9:52
Sent disciples out and empowered them to achieve the Great Commission; the power of prayer	Empowering broad-based action	Matthew 10 Luke 10–16 Mark 6:7–13
Performed miracles	Generating short-term wins	Mark 1:29–34, 40–42
Repeatedly in Acts, the ongoing success of the church's mission is stressed in summaries that mark its progress: Christians succeed not only in being faithful disciples themselves but also in "turning the world upside down" in having a transforming effect on society. Numerous stories present the church as triumphant over all forms of evil, wiping out poverty, healing diseases.	Consolidation gains and producing more change	Acts: 1:14; 2:41; 4:4; 5:14; 6:7; 9:31; 11:21, 24; 12:24; 14:1; 16:5; 19:20; 28:30–31 Acts 17:6 Acts 4:32–37 Acts 5:12–16 Luke 10:17–18

Jesus's Change Process	Kotter's Eight-Stage Process	Relevant Bible Verse(s)
Disciples/apostles get out the word; creation of the New Testament, including the four Gospels; prioritizing actions	Anchoring new approaches in the culture	Matthew 6

Your Christ-Inspired Leadership Bible Verses

ENDNOTES

Introduction

[1] Megan Brenan and Nicole Willcoxon, "Record-High 50% of Americans Rate U.S. Moral Values as 'Poor,'" Gallup, June 15, 2022, https://news.gallup.com/poll/393659/record-high-americans-rate-moral-values-poor.aspx.

[2] Jeffery M Jones, "Belief in God in U.S. Dips to 81%, a New Low," Gallup, June 17, 2022, https://news.gallup.com/poll/393737/belief-god-dips-new-low.aspx?version=print.

[3] David Ignatius, "Opinion: Nearly Every American Has a Foreboding the Country They Love Is Losing Its Way," *Washington Post*, July 3, 2022, https://www.washingtonpost.com/opinions/2022/07/03/july-4-america-national-character-decline.

1

[1] Francis Collins, *The Language of God: A Scientist Presents Evidence for Belief* (Free Press, 2008).

[2] Peter Manseau, *The Jefferson Bible: A Biography. The Life and Times of a Uniquely American Testament* (Princeton University Press, September 2020).

[3] Ross Gregory Douthat, *Bad Religion: How We Became a Nation of Heretics* (Free Press, April 2012).

[4] Kristen Kobes Du Mez, *Jesus and John Wayne. How White Evangelicals Corrupted a Faith and Fractured a Nation* (Liveright, June 2020).

[5] Jason Duaine Hahn, "Aaron Rodgers Opens Up about Religion to Danica Patrick: 'I Don't Know How You Can Believe in God,'" *People* magazine, January 22, 2020, https://people.com/sports/aaron-rodgers-opens-up-about-religion-to-danica-patrick-i-dont-know-how-you-can-believe-in-a-god/#:~:text=%E2%80%9CI%20don't%20know%20how,the%20end%20of%20all%20this%3F%E2%80%9D.

6   Peter Enns, *The Sin of Certainty: Why God Desires Our Trust More Than Our "Correct" Beliefs* (HarperOne, April 2016).

7   Heidi Schlumpf, "Sr. Joan Chittister's 2004 Quote on 'Pro-Life' versus 'Pro-Birth' Goes Viral," *National Catholic Reporter*, May 23, 2019, https://www.ncronline.org/news/politics/sr-joan-chittisters-2004-quote-pro-life-versus-pro-birth-goes-viral.

8   Diana Butler Bass, *Freeing Jesus: Rediscovering Jesus as Friend, Teacher, Savior, Lord, Way, and Presence* (HarperOne, March 2021).

9   *Luther in Real Time*, podcast, Ligonier Ministries.

10   A.W. Tozer, "Preaching: Deadly Rationalizism. Tozer on Leadership," https://www.biblegateway.com/devotionals/tozer-on-leadership/2042/05/10.

2

1   Pew Research Center, "America's Abortion Quandary," May 2022.

2   Francis Collins, *The Language of God: A Scientist Presents Evidence for Belief* (Free Press, July 2006).

3   Francis S. Collins, *The Language of God: A Scientist Presents Evidence for Belief* (Free Press, July 2006).

4   Josh McDowell, *Evidence That Demands a Verdict* (Thomas Nelson, October 2017).

5   Sydney Harris, cartoon, "Then a Miracle Occurs."

3

1   Jaroslav Pelikan, *Jesus through the Centuries* (Yale University Press, November 1999).

4

1   A.W. Tozer, "The Holy Spirit: Wild-Eyed Fanatics," Tozer on Leadership, https://www.biblegateway.com/devotionals/tozer-on-leadership/2028/02/13.

2   Ben Kirby, https://preachersnsneakers.com/.

3   Dwight L. Moody, multiple sources.

4   John Milton, *Lycidas*.

5   David French, "How American Christendom Weakens American Christianity," *French Press*, May 9, 2021, https://frenchpress.thedispatch.com/p/how-american-christendom-weakens?s=r.

5

[1] Jim Collins, Good to Great and the Social Sectors: Why Business Thinking Is Not the Answer (HarperCollins, November 2005).

6

[1] Victor Strecher, Life on Purpose: How Living for What Matters Most Changes Everything (HarperOne, May 2016).

[2] Harris Poll, "One quarter of full-time workers experienced food insecurity," https://www.bayer.com/en/us/new-survey-reveals-increased-concerns-over-food-insecurity-in-us.

[3] Richard Boyatzis, Annie McKee, Daniel Goleman, "Reawakening Your Passion for Work," *Harvard Business Review*, April 2002.

[4] Jerry Liver and Mike Stoller, "Is That All There Is?"

[5] Max De Pree, *Leadership Is an Art* (Currency, June 2011).

[6] William D. Edwards, Wesley Gabel, Floyd Hosmer, "On the Physical Death of Jesus Christ," *JAMA* 255, no. 11 (1986):1455–1463, doi:10:10.1101/jama.1986.03370110077725.

7

[1] Jim Collins, Good to Great and the Social Sectors: Why Business Thinking Is Not the Answer (HarperCollins, November 2005).

[2] Cindy Wooden, "Pope Offers New Beatitudes for Saints of a New Age," *Catholic News*, November 2016, https://cruxnow.com/vatican/2016/11/01/pope-francis-offers-new-beatitudes-saints-new-age.

[3] KPMG, "KPMG 2020 CEO Outlook," https://home.kpmg/xx/en/home/insights/2020/09/kpmg-2020-ceo-outlook-covid-19-special-edition.html.

[4] Wikipedia, "Friedman doctrine," https://en.wikipedia.org/wiki/Friedman_doctrine#:~:text=Friedman%20introduced%20the%20theory%20in,responsibility%20is%20to%20its%20shareholders.

[5] Business Roundtable, "Business Roundtable Redefines the Purpose of a Corporation to Promote an Economy That Serves All Americans," August 2019, https://www.businessroundtable.org/business-roundtable-redefines-the-purpose-of-a-corporation-to-promote-an-economy-that-serves-all-americans.

[6] T. S. Eliot, *Four Quartets. East Coker,* https://en.wikipedia.org/wiki/Four_Quartets.

8

1   Robert Greenleaf, The Servant as Leader (1970), https://www.greenleaf.org/products-page/the-servant-as-leader/.

2   Deborah Ancona, Thomas W. Malone, Wanda J. Orlikowski, Peter M. Senge, "In Praise of the Incomplete Leader," Harvard Business Review, February 2007, https://hbr.org/2007/02/in-praise-of-the-incomplete-leader.

3   Max De Pree, Leadership Is an Art, Leadership Jazz, and Leadership without Power.

4   Ibid.

5   Wikipedia, "John Woolman," https://en.wikipedia.org/wiki/John_Woolman.

6   Peter Sczaaero, Emotionally Healthy Discipleship: Moving from Shallow Christianity to Deep Transformation (Zondervan, March 2021).

9

1   John Kotter, Leading Change (Harvard Business Review Press, October 2012).

2   Jaroslav Pelikan, Jesus through the Centuries: His Place in the History of Culture (Yale University Press, 1999).

3   Mark S. Granovetter, "The Strength of Weak Ties," American Journal of Sociology 78, no. 6 (1973): 1360–80, http://www.jstor.org/stable/2776392.

10

1   Daniel Goleman, Emotional Intelligence—Why It Can Matter More Than IQ (Random House Publishing Group, September 2005).

2   Eillie Anzilotti, "What Happened When New Yorkers Scribbled Their Biggest Regrets on a Blackboard," Bloomberg, February 4, 2016, https://www.bloomberg.com/news/articles/2016-02-04/new-yorkers-write-their-biggest-regrets-on-a-blackboard-in-a-lower-manhattan-park.

3   Clayton M Christensen, "How Will You Measure Your Life?" Harvard Business Review (July/August 2010), https://hbr.org/2010/07/how-will-you-measure-your-life.

4   Patrick Reyes, The Purpose Gap (Westminister John Know Press, March 2021).

5   Carol Dweck, "What Having a 'Growth Mindset' Actually Means," Harvard Business Review (January 13, 2016), https://hbr.org/2016/01/what-having-a-growth-mindset-actually-means.

11

[1] Attributed to multiple sources, including Mozart, DeBussy, Yo-Yo Ma, and others.

[2] Robert Putnam, *Bowling Alone: The Collapse and Revival of American Community* (Simon & Schuster, anniversary edition, August 2001).

12

[1] Elizabeth Bernstein, "The Science of Prayer," Wall Street Journal, May 17, 2020, https://www.wsj.com/articles/the-science-of-prayer-11589720400

[2] Ibid.

[3] Gretchen Ronnevik, *Ragged: Spiritual Disciplines for the Spiritually Exhausted* (1517 Publishing, May 2021).

[4] Rick Warren, *The Purpose Driven Life: What on Earth Am I here For?* (Zondervan, 10th edition, October 2012).

[5] Daniel Goleman, *Emotional Intelligence—Why It Can Matter More Than IQ* (Random House Publishing Group, September 2005).

13

[1] R.C. Sproul, "A Simple Acrostic for prayer: A.C.T.S.," June 23, 2018. https://www.ligonier.org/learn/articles/simple-acrostic-prayer.

[2] Clayton M Christensen, "How Will You Measure Your Life?" *Harvard Business Review* (July/August 2010), https://hbr.org/2010/07/how-will-you-measure-your-life.

Printed in the United States
by Baker & Taylor Publisher Services